REAL MONEY REAL ESTATE

Winning the Real Estate game.

9780958093262

W0010683

By
BRADLEY J. SUGARS
with David Hows & Phil Jones

Edited By Grant Mc Duling

ACTION International Pty Ltd

i

ISBN 0958093261
FIRST EDITION

Published by *ACTION International* Pty Ltd
GPO Box 1340 Brisbane, QLD 4001
Phone: +61 (0) 7 3368 2525
Fax: +61 (0) 7 3368 2535
www.action-international.com

Distributed by *ACTION International* for further information
contact +61 (0) 7 3368 2525

Printed in Australia by Pure Print

To those who trusted enough to invest,
the future is yours ...

▮ Acknowledgments

As an investor and entrepreneur, it's hard to take time out to put together a book, let alone a book that gives people enough information to get them flying. That's why I have to thank a great team of people.

Firstly to Phil and David, you are shining examples of the fact that sometimes the student can teach the teacher. You are both fantastic examples of what can be achieved with what we've written here in this book and what we teach every day.

To Grant, my infamous editor who makes my words and work make sense. Thanks for your dedication to the cause.

To my students, you know who you are; you've helped me refine what we teach, you've asked questions that made me remember why we do certain things and you've had the courage to live the dream.

To my teachers, and there have been many, a very big thank-you for teaching this businessman that maybe property isn't so boring after all.

To the teams at **ACTION International** and the Entrepreneurs Success Centre, every day you make people's lives better without even knowing it. Remember that and enjoy the hard work; it's what makes the differnece ...

And lastly to my wife Jennifer ... you are the one who gives me the strength to not only do this every day, but to put myself out there and teach others how it can be done. You do the most important things.

■ CONTENTS

▌Introduction

> Man was born to be rich, or grow rich by use of his faculties, by the union of thought with nature. Property is an intellectual production. The game requires coolness, right reasoning, promptness, and patience in the players. Cultivated labour drives out brute labour.
>
> *Ralph Waldo Emerson (1803 - 1882)*

Everyone understands you can make money investing in Real Estate. Everyone understands that property is one of the best forms of investment available. And it doesn't matter in which city you invest; the results speak for themselves. It doesn't even matter in which country you buy property –investors the world over all tell a similar story.

Why then do relatively few people choose property as an investment medium? Is it due to the high entry costs? Is it because most people can't even afford to buy their own home, let alone a property purely for its longer-term investment potential?

Or is it that most 'ordinary' people find it too confusing, too difficult to understand and too risky?

If you fit into any of these categories, then sit back, relax and read on…you're in for a huge surprise. We're going to teach you everything you need to know about developing wealth through Real Estate. We're going to reveal to you all the tricks of the trade, all the pitfalls and all the secrets insiders like Phil, David and myself have used to make millions of dollars buying residential property. That's right, millions.

We currently own residential property across multiple counties and all over those countries. And it would be true to say we wouldn't even have a clue where they all are. But each and every one was bought for a purpose – to produce either capital growth or an income stream so that we don't have to work.

Introduction

We, between us, built or rebuilt hundreds of properties and currently have property portfolios worth many millions of dollars. I have a bunch of properties valued from less than $60,000 each right up to single properties worth many millions alone. And at least one of everything in between.

We all have a strategy for wealth creation, and we stick to it! We build cashflow or income through our various business, property and stock market investments, and then invest the profits into Real Estate. We follow a formula that doesn't fail us.

This book has not been written to show you how to buy four or five properties in a lifetime, but rather how to become a *property millionaire well within ten years*. It's about buying four or five properties a year, not in a lifetime! You see, what's the point of retiring owning just four or five investment properties when all that means, in reality, is that you'd earn too much to draw a social pension, yet not enough to finance a decent lifestyle for the many years to come?

This book is about getting results. It's about **ACTION**. It is based on real experiences and real examples. It contains charts and formulae that you can put to good use RIGHT NOW.

But perhaps more importantly, this book is simple to understand. It is based on knowledge we have acquired over the years. And it's tested knowledge - knowledge we have used ourselves for great personal reward.

This knowledge has been distilled so it's easy to understand and use straight away. So please, consider this book your personal coach because through it, we will be imparting INVALUABLE knowledge about how to win the Real Estate Game.

If you do take it on board, we know you can win. We have coached literally thousands of people through seminars and coaching sessions, and most of them have been able to realise their wildest dreams through the knowledge they've learnt and put into **ACTION**.

▮ Making It Easy To Understand

A child of five would understand this. Send someone to fetch a child of five.

Groucho Marx

Real Money Real Estate has been written so it's easy to understand. It has been written for ordinary, everyday people with little or no understanding of how to go about investing in residential property. Yet it's still extremely valuable and full of single hints and tips that will give even the most experienced investor a better Return On Investment (ROI).

Some of the concepts you'll read about may seem simple and some will be common sense. Some will also be quite the opposite of what many investment experts advise. But what you are about to learn works. It's been developed, tried and tested over a 35-year period, then tweaked, fine-tuned, and honed. The result is, we believe, the MOST POWERFUL, easy-to-UNDERSTAND and easy-to-IMPLEMENT recipe for wealth creation and financial freedom you'll ever come across.

It all begins with having the right attitude. Like anything in life, if you have the wrong attitude, you'll get nowhere. You need the right frame of mind to succeed. You need to see things in a certain light.

What we're about to teach you will certainly be enlightening.

The first part of the book deals with getting you to understand the WHY of investing in Real Estate. Why you should do this, why the system works and why so few people understand the rules of the game. The second part deals with the HOW. How the rules work, how you can use the principle of leverage to your best advantage, and how you can generate amazing wealth through implementing some of the tips and techniques you will learn about. Understand this: the second part of the book will be meaningless unless you grasp the first part.

You will truly see how easy investing in Real Estate can be, how much fun it can be, and how rewarding it can be.

Making it easy to understand

This book covers not only the attitudinal requirements necessary to succeed; it also explains the so-called technical aspects of the game – 'the rules'.

It is littered with real-life examples to illustrate in simple, easy-to-understand terms the various aspects and concepts involved.

Throughout the book, we will also be giving you tips and rules that are not generally freely available. We will be passing on knowledge gained through a lifetime of work in the real estate industry.

So, what are we waiting for? Let's get started…

PART 1

▮ Victor Or Victim?

> Self-reverence, self-knowledge, self-control; these three alone lead life to sovereign power.
>
> *Alfred Lord Tennyson*

It's now time to reflect on some of the things you need to know to succeed, not only in your business life, but in your private life as well. They are certainly relevant when it comes to investing in Real Estate.

Let's get imaginative for a while. There is an imaginary line that separates people into two basic categories. Think of it as a horizontal line.

People play the game – and it can be any game – below the line or above it.

Ownership
Accountable
Responsible

VICTOR

Blame
Excuses
Denial

VICTIM

The first thing those who play below line do is to BLAME other people. They come up with EXCUSES. They DENY what they are doing or what is going on. They blame the economy for their poor performance in business, they use their difficult boss as an excuse for their lack of progress, or they deny their marriage break-up had anything to do with them. If this sounds like someone you know, it means they are playing the role of a VICTIM.

Those who play above the line say, "OK, let's take OWNERSHIP of our situation. Let's take RESPONSIBILITY for our actions. Let's be ACCOUNTABLE. If you play above the line, you're basically taking responsibility for your life. You're saying you're accountable for your results. You're saying you're not a VICTIM; you're a VICTOR. You're saying you're in charge of your life.

You might be surprised to learn that 95% of people live their lives below the line.

> Most people just bumble along blaming others for their lot in life. Most people go through life in denial. If they want to succeed, they've got to shift into the zone above the line. That may take a quantum shift in their belief patterns. It may also require them to challenge the way they view life. But they have to do *whatever it takes* if they want to take control of their lives; once they assume responsibility, they'll be amazed at how they suddenly start making progress towards achieving the things they previously only dreamed of – and so can YOU!

One other key point to achieving success is allowing yourself to fail every now and then. Allow yourself to make mistakes. If you are not willing to once in a while, you won't try new things. Instead, every time you try something new, you'll throw your hands up and say, "Slow down, that's far enough. Don't go any further." The ability to fail is the sign of a true leader. Just remember, when (and not if) you fail, don't get into 'I won't do that again' mode. Instead look at what you need to modify to make it work next time.

We are all human. Often the difference between a VICTOR and a VICTIM is not the number of failures we have, but how we have chosen to deal with them. A VICTOR takes control of their life; a VICTIM lets life control them.

Remember, perfection leads to pain and standing still. Strive for excellence – be a Victor and enjoy the financial abundance your winning attitude will bring.

Success is the constant process of moving toward your goals no matter what obstacles life throws in your way.

Play above the line, take control of your financial future and make it all it can be.

There are no Rich Victims,
only Rich Victors.

▍ Left Brain, Right Brain And The Learning Process

> That is what learning is. You suddenly understand something you've understood all your life, but in a new way.
>
> *Doris Lessing*

Now think about your brain and the processes that allow you to do things. No, the aim here isn't to make Real Estate a more confusing subject than many believe it is. The idea is to actually dispel a few myths and set you on the path to success right from the word go.

You probably already know that the brain is divided into two halves. These are known as the left brain and the right brain. The left brain controls our logic while the right brain looks after creative thought processes. Most of us don't allow both halves to function simultaneously, but we all have the ability. And why does the Real Estate Investor need to use both sides of the brain? Easy. The numbers and words and logic are left brain factors. But you need the right side – the creative – to see how to put the deal together, to see what others don't. All it takes is practice.

For most of us, when the left and right brains work simultaneously we learn and make decisions rapidly. However, generally prior to learning something new, we need to experience some level of confusion. Now confusion in itself isn't a bad thing because it makes your brain work in a higher state – it has to work out what is going on in addition to running all its usual tasks and processes.

The challenge is that when most people experience confusion, they just say, "I don't know." If you're ever going to be successful, you have to learn that confusion means it's time to ask a new question – a better question; then you'll move forward.

But let's go back a little. What we do know is that in our first five years of life we learn the most. We learn everything from walking and talking to discovering as much about our immediate environment as we can. We learn to recognize people, how to react to certain situations and what is good and what is not. From then until about the age of 16, we settle into thought and behavioural patterns that will stay with us for the rest of our lives. We develop habits that can become very difficult, but not impossible, to change later on.

But, change habits we must. If you're going to create wealth at all, you have to learn difficult things, think a different way and therefore do different things.

It's impossible to create wealth without learning new things.

So, how do we learn new things?

Just because you didn't succeed at something doesn't mean you are a failure. You see, the only real failure in life is the failure to participate.

Remember back to when you learned to ride a bike. You probably had someone stand behind you, holding the seat to balance for you as you started to pedal. You probably wobbled all the way down the driveway at first, safe in the knowledge that someone was supporting you. Then, after a few attempts, you turned around to ask a question, only to find they weren't there. They were standing up at the top of the driveway watching you with a big smile on their face.

Then you promptly lost confidence and fell over.

Did you give up there and then? No, of course not. You climbed back onto your bike and tried again, only this time you made sure someone ran behind you with their reassuring hand firmly holding the saddle. However, the time came when they let go and you were able to stay upright on your own. Now think harder – can you remember exactly when they let go of the saddle? Probably not. All you may remember is rejoicing in the fact that you could ride. What an exhilarating feeling that was! From that moment on, you could ride unaided. And it was a moment you'd never forget.

Learning is all about taking some sort of **ACTION**. You have to do something. It's not a passive process. We can give you **EDUCATION** through this book, or at a seminar, but you still have to learn by doing.

Understand this: Give a person a fish and you'll feed them for a day. Teach that person to fish and you feed them for a lifetime.

The aim of this book is to teach you how to fish for wealth through Real Estate. We're not suggesting you can't get rich through the stock market or business – we've done very well indeed through both of them ourselves. We've also made millions through Real Estate, and that's what we want to teach you.

We're going to teach you some interesting tactics that work. You'll learn some strategies and different ways of doing things. By the time you reach the end of this book, you will have sufficient knowledge to go out and make it happen. You'll have been taught the hottest ideas, tips and strategies necessary to become extremely wealthy through Real Estate. We're not talking about a get rich quick scheme either. We're talking about a three to ten-year process to becoming rich. It will allow you to retire in that time and you can certainly become extremely wealthy in ten years. It's that simple. We're talking about a process that is so simple anyone can achieve fantastic results, but you have to work at it – you have to learn and do.

But right now, there's something else you must know that's extremely important.

> We believe the most dangerous two words in the English language are the words **I know**.

If somebody tells you something, and you say, "I know," your brain goes into filter mode. You see, because of the amount of information it is being constantly bombarded with, it tries to avoid overload and filters out what it already knows or has. It discards surplus information. The problem is, generally, it's what you 'know' that really isn't correct and this stops you from succeeding.

At one time, people really 'knew' the sun revolved around the earth. They were absolutely convinced this was a 'fact' and the rest of their knowledge and reasoning was based on this assumption. Until Galileo (1564 – 1642) appeared on the scene, that is. This forward thinker became well-known for thinking outside the square. In 1630, he published his views about the orbital motion of the earth around the sun. It changed the world forever.

We would suggest you banish the phrase **I know** from your vocabulary and replace it with either, "As I understand just now," or "What I believe right now." This creates two improvements: it makes your brain function at a higher level, and if, at a later time, you discover you were not quite right, you won't go into self-destruct mode – you'll need only to change a belief or increase your understanding of the situation.

Let's now consider the words **knowledge** and **wisdom**. What's the difference between them?

Having knowledge means being able to relate something you've just heard to something you already understand. Having wisdom means understanding both how and when to apply that knowledge.

Understand this: you can have all the knowledge in the world, but if you don't do something with it, you end up with nothing at all. You need to apply it; you need to take **ACTION** to achieve results.

For you to truly learn how to become rich through property, you have to add to what you know, and in most cases, totally edit (that is remove) some of your old thinking and replace it with entirely new thoughts.

It's all about attitude. It's about what you're thinking. If you're broke, it's only because you're broke in your mind. If you're wealthy, you have to be wealthy in your mind first. Some people just don't believe this, but if you do, it'll make a HUGE difference.

You have to understand your mind is a very powerful thing and it'll give you everything you want out of life. The challenge for most people is they just don't believe this. They don't understand how to use their mental faculties to make things happen for them.

So, why is this so important in a book about Real Estate? Simple. Most of the deals we do, anyone could have done. It's just that they thought poor, so they didn't see the rich deals.

Ever heard the saying that positive thought leads to positive action? Well the same is true in Real Estate. Rich thoughts lead to rich actions, or, put bluntly, you need to think rich to be rich. Throughout this book, we will teach you about both thinking and doing rich. You need both!

▌ Investing

> Lack of money is the root of all evil.
>
> *George Bernard Shaw (1856 - 1950)*

Why Invest?

There are some very powerful reasons for investing. Some of them are obvious, others not. Let's begin with a few sobering statistics.

Statistics tell us that, of 100 Australians aged 25 today, at age 65 ...

1 will be RICH ...

4 will be INDEPENDENT ...

5 will still be WORKING ...

27 will be DEAD ...

63 will be FLAT BROKE ...

It wasn't that most of these people planned to fail; they just FAILED TO PLAN.

 Let's look at what the statistics say for America. The following facts exist for every 100 people at age 65.

25 are DEAD

20 have annual incomes UNDER $6,000 (below the poverty level)

51 have annual incomes BETWEEN $6,000 AND $35,000 (average is $12,000)

4 have annual incomes OVER $35,000

Here's some more interesting information about these facts:

- Today's average 50-year-old has only $2,300 saved towards their retirement. (J. Urcivloi, Snr VP Merrill Lynch)
- Only 5% of the population can put their hands on $10,000 when they are 65.

- When Social Security was started there were 16 people working for every one person on the program.
- Today the ratio is 3:1
- In the next 12 years it is projected to be 1:1, maybe...

This raises another interesting point. When is it appropriate to measure success? At graduation, or at retirement? A very good question indeed.

The sad thing about these statistics is that 95% of us are basically living in poverty. And it doesn't seem to matter which country we look at or even what period of time we draw the statistics from, the picture remains the same. Admittedly, these days we are living longer than we did 30 years ago, yet we're only just becoming more financially literate. We're not being taught how to manage our money even though the need to do so is greater now than ever before.

Looking at these statistics, it is clear this has to change. It all depends on our thought processes – we can simply change what we do and how we do it.

These figures show that 95% of us are planning a life of poverty. We are planning to retire on a pension that will barely give us the means to eke out a meagre existence in our twilight years.

But there are those who say they're investing for their future by buying a property, paying it off, buying another, paying it off and so on until they have three or four properties. That's fine, if what they want to do is to own three or four properties. It's about all the average person can realistically achieve in their working lives by using this method.

But think about what this strategy will deliver. It will result in an income stream that is not much better than what you'd get on a pension. The downside is you wouldn't have the benefits the pension would give.

Wouldn't it be far better to acquire three or four properties every year? This way, you certainly would be planning on becoming part of that wealthy segment of the population.

Impossible? Read on...

It's all entirely possible, simply because of a principle Albert Einstein said was one of the most amazing phenomena of the universe – compound interest.

That's right. Compound interest.

If you understand the concept of compound interest, you'll understand why Real Estate works so well as an investment medium.

When you first start out using compound interest, all the hard work takes place up front, at the beginning. Then, as time goes on, you reach a stage where its critical mass kicks in and things get easier. It becomes self-perpetuating. Your investment will grow under its own steam. The challenge for most people is working hard enough and sticking with it during the initial stages.

As an example, imagine you could start an investment with just 1c at the beginning of the month. Imagine too that this small investment were to double in value each and every day until the end of the month. The hard work would take place during the early stages until it hits its critical mass. Let me show you:

On day two your investment would be worth 2c, on day three 4c, day four 8c, day five 16c and on day six 32c. What would it be worth half way through the month on day 15? Only $163.84.

OK, now here's the interesting part. What do you reckon it would be worth at the end of the month, on day 31?

A staggering $10,737,418.24.

That's over ten million dollars! That's also a very graphic illustration of the compounding effect.

So what does all this mean to you?

Let's assume the average person works for about 30 years. When should they start investing? When their children are off their hands? Now there's nothing wrong with starting late in life, but think of the cost. You see, it's not the cost upfront that is horrendous; it's what they are losing out on at the end that really is staggering.

On the 30th day of the month above, you had only $5 million – just half.

Understand this: in Real Estate, the longer you hang on to a property, the more it'll be worth. Real Estate is all about two things: rate and time. Rate, of course, refers to the rate of return, or the return on your invested capital, and we all know what time is.

Investing

Does that mean you should use this as an excuse if you're already a little older? No way. You should use it as a reason to work harder, to get more knowledge and to do whatever it takes to reach your goals.

■ The 6 Levels Of The Real Estate Investor

So often I meet people who say they're into Real Estate. What do they mean? You see, as with anything in life, there are different 'levels' of investing in Real Estate. Many people will tell you they play sport, but at what level? The same applies to being an investor.

Just owning a piece of Real Estate won't necessarily make you rich. Well, it might if it happened to be an acre or two on the lawn of the White House or at Sydney Harbour overlooking the Opera House and the Sydney Harbour Bridge. But what I'm talking about is owning a home or two in an average suburb. Think of it this way – by just doing some basic exercises every day, you wouldn't expect to qualify for the Olympics. There are specific strategies and skills you'll need to turn your Real Estate investment dreams into reality.

I've always believed that investing in Real Estate is like playing a game. If you want to play the game, you'd better learn the rules. What's more, learn them from someone who's succeeded at the game and not from the scorekeepers (accountants), the rule makers (lawyers), the spectators (friends and family), the money holders and collectors (bankers), and definitely not from 'D'grade players (the average home owner). You've got to learn from the best players and coaches you can find.

It seems so obvious when you consider it from this point of view, doesn't it? But this raises another question – who are best people to learn from? But before I answer that, I want to remind you of something. Most people who fail in Real Estate always find excuses for their failure, whereas the ones who succeed take responsibility for all their actions. They are in control of their lives.

Now, let's take a closer look at the different types of the Real Estate Investor. You'll notice there are 6 levels. I've included Level 0 because this is where the vast majority of people are, even though they're not really investors at all.

- **Level 0:** Those who are renting their homes.
- **Level 1:** Those who own their own home or are paying it off.
- **Level 2:** Those who have a negatively geared investment property.
- **Level 3:** Those who own income-producing property that pays for itself.
- **Level 4:** Those who are full-time residential Real Estate investors.

The 6 levels of the real estate investor

- **Level 5:** Commercial Real Estate investors
- **Level 6:** Property developers.

The aim of this book is to take you to Level 4.

Level 0: Those who are renting their homes.

Almost everyone starts out here. Many remain tenants all their lives, but others save up for their first property while renting. And these days, renting has become a lifestyle option for some. They reason the money 'saved' by not buying a property could be better spent on other forms of investment. That's highly debatable.

It's our view that the one sure way to wealth lies through investing in Real Estate, and for good reason. You see, the government's not about to provide housing for the ever-increasing number of people who have no option but to rent their accommodation. That's left to people like us – the investors. Indeed, if it weren't for the fact that more and more people are looking for rental accommodation, Real Estate might not be such a great investment option. Furthermore, as those tenants who are renting while saving to buy their first home begin looking for their first Real Estate deal, it's from Level 4 and 6 investors like us that they'll most probably buy. And when they do, they'll move up to Level 1.

Level 1: Those who own their own home or are paying it off.

This is the first step up the ladder - the first step towards creating wealth through Real Estate ownership. Owning your own home is most people's Great Dream – it's what we all aim for. And having a roof over your head is one of the most basic of human needs.

Most people aim at ensuring their home is paid for by the time they retire. This relieves them of one major burden in their golden years – having to come up with the money to pay the mortgage.

Of course, many also aspire to owning their own home as it gives them a sense of belonging, of sinking their roots, of permanence. It also gives them a sense of worth.

But more importantly, as time goes by, it gives owners a means of progressing to the next level through being able to access equity funds. It allows them to purchase their first investment property.

Level 2: Those who have a negatively geared investment property.

Welcome to the first real entrepreneurial level of the Real Estate Investor. That's right, you see, Level 1 is really only the beginning, but it's also really the level at which you take care of your own housing needs and not those of others. Level 2 is where you really begin operating as a Real Estate Investor as it's here you'll be focusing on generating some sort of income through property ownership.

Many people take their first step into the world of investment property ownership through buying a negatively geared property. These are the ones that make a paper or cash loss and they are useful, especially if you have highly taxable sources of income.

But I would never buy a property purely for the tax benefits it produces because depreciation-based tax savings dissipate over time – there must be other, sounder, reasons to make any Real Estate investment attractive. It must produce longer-term capital growth or meet our wealth creation goals.

For many, the real aim would be to progress to the next level as soon as possible.

Level 3: Those who own income-producing property that pays for itself.

The real attraction of owning an investment property lies in the fact that the tenant will be paying off your investment, which, as time goes by, will be increasing in value. The investor scores on two fronts.

At this level, you'll be reaping a positive cashflow (pre-tax) from your investment property, with the rental income you receive being greater than the expenses you incur through owning it. The beauty here is you receive both passive income and taxation deductions through depreciation and other expenses – a very nice win!

It's at this level that you'll really begin to see the advantages of investing in Real Estate. You'll really begin to experience the power of leverage. You'll discover how easy it is to grow your portfolio and you'll thirst for more. You'll begin seeing the advantages of progressing to the next level.

Level 4: Those who are full-time Real Estate investors.

It is at this level where you earn enough from your investment properties to be able to quit your job. You'll operate here as a full-time Real Estate investor, being able to rely solely on the proceeds your investment properties produce.

The 6 levels of the real estate investor

At this level, you'll need to structure your affairs in such a way as to provide you with the maximum amount of protection, while at the same time ensuring the long-term viability of your portfolio. You'll be concerned with factors such as financial and legal structures (asset planning), diversification strategies (spreading the risk of your property portfolio), market variations (finding out where the best deals are) and management.

You will invest in a range of Real Estate both inter-country and inter-state and operate with a degree of sophistication, intimately understanding and using tools like quick cash deals, wraps, property options, renovations and many others.

Level 5: Commercial Real Estate investors

Many level 4 investors are naturally drawn to this level where bigger deals and bigger challenges await.

Caution: Savvy commercial sharks prowl these waters awaiting fresh newbie investor meat. Don't swim with the big fish until you are very ready. It's not a nice feeling being shark food!

The rules of the level 5 game are different to levels 1 to 4 and the intelligence and sophistication of operators in this market is considerable.

We never have more than 15% to 25% of our total property portfolios in commercial property and we would strongly recommend you do the same. The 1987 Stock Market crash wiped out many commercial investors because they didn't spread their risk or balance their portfolios with appropriate proportions of residential property.

History will repeat itself. When it does, be ready.

It's not the intention of this book to discuss this level in any depth.

Level 6: Property developers.

It's at this level where you'd become actively involved in developing property from scratch – developments like cluster homes, townhouse complexes, unit developments, shopping centres or estates. Those who operate here are the big operators; the people who take major risks but see serious returns for their efforts.

It's not the intention of this book to discuss this level in any depth.

▮ Seven Fundamental Steps To Creating Wealth

> If you can count your money, you don't have a billion dollars.
>
> *J. Paul Getty*

The Seven Fundamental Steps To Creating Wealth are just that. They are FUNDAMENTAL. They are the steps that must be followed and up on which everything that follows depends. They serve as the starting point to wealth.

These fundamental rules are not new. They have been around in various forms and guises for as long as man has been using money. They are simple, straight-forward and easily achievable.

So what are they?

Step #1 ... Accumulate Investment Capital

A high income does not equal wealth – it's not how much you make, but how much you SAVE that makes the difference. Also SAVE to invest, don't save to SPEND later. The challenge lies with our upbringing. You see, we were brought up being taught to save something from our weekly pocket money so we could buy those big items we couldn't ordinarily afford. And it made sense at the time. Most people still teach their children this. We should rather be teaching them not to save, but to invest. It's a fact that if we were to invest just 10% of everything we earned from the time we started working, we'd be able to retire within 15 years.

Step # 2 ... Control Your Expenditure

It's not how much you take in, but how much you pay out that will send you broke. The easiest way to control how much you spend is to budget. Take what you need to invest off what you earn before anything else. Then live off what is left. Work out your regular expenses as a percentage of what you earn, and learn to stick within those percentages. As your income increases, so can your living standards.

For instance, you might find your car represents 15% of your income, your home 25%, your health 3%, food 7% and so on. Learn to live within these percentages. If you find your spending patterns drift, you'll know you're not living well, and you'll need to take remedial action.

> **Remember this**: it's the monthly repayments where you borrow to pay for a holiday, furniture or even a car that seem a good way to buy but will end up keeping you poor.

Ever heard of the saying: *A penny saved is a penny earned?* Well, don't believe a word of it. You see, a penny saved and properly invested is about 5 or 10 pennies earned.

> Understand this: if you run a business and decided to cut costs by just 1%, where would that saved 1% end up? Straight on your bottom-line. Now if your business were making a 10% profit, that 1% would actually equate to a 10% increase to your bottom-line. That's pretty dramatic in anyone's language.

It's the little things that count. I find that by tightening up on the vacancy factors on all my properties, the savings together are enough to buy a new unit every year. Isn't that incredible? The savings may be small individually, but added together they make a huge difference.

And if we can do it, so can you!

Step #3 ... Invest Your Accumulated Capital

Remember, anything worthwhile takes time. Don't get frustrated and pull your accumulated capital out just when it's starting to work. The most difficult period in any investment is the initial stage before critical mass kicks in. It's like pushing a car. Just to get it moving takes considerable effort, but once it starts rolling, it gets easier and easier until eventually it will roll all by itself. Investments are just the same. It's all about the effects of compounding interest.

Step #4 ... Protect Your Capital

By this I don't mean you must lock your capital up. The adage *If it sounds too good to be true, it most probably is*, sums up Step #4 beautifully.

Remember, the main criterion for an investment is still Return 'OF' Investment, before Return 'ON' Investment. We so often lose sight of this, as the greed factor tends to get the better of us. We must always weigh up whether we are likely to get our money back when evaluating any investment option.

Step #5 ... Consider Your Home As A Profitable Investment

Your home will provide you with probably the cheapest money you'll ever get. Use the equity in your home. Security isn't gained by tying up your largest asset. Many people simply don't understand that using the equity in their home is very different to risking it.

There are many ways to safeguard your security. Here's just one. (Example only: Not intended as investment advice.)

Let's suppose you have a house worth $500,000 which is mortgage free. Let's also suppose you are keen to invest in a high risk Real Estate venture called DumbDurks where for $1,000,000 you are going to build a movie cinema in a desert 300 km from anywhere.

To offer your house as security for the DumbDurks investment would be plain stupid. What would happen if the deal went belly up? You could lose your home and possibly the shirt off your back!

What some people do is to set up a Trust (or similar structure as recommended by your accountant or an asset planning expert), then raise a mortgage on their home to the value of the available equity (lets say $400,000) and then invest these funds in a fixed-term deposit. The $400,000 in the fixed-term deposit is then used as security for a bank to provide a mortgage of $1,000,000 (40% or $400,000 secured against the fixed-deposit account and 60% or $600,000 secured against the DumbDurks property) to purchase the DumbDurks property.

This way, if the deal collapses, the only risk to the homeowner is the loss of the $400,000 invested in the fixed-term deposit.

The home is protected by both the Trust and the fact that the mortgage advanced by the bank (to purchase DumbDurks) is not secured against the investor's home but against the fixed deposit. The result? The investor's home remains isolated from the DumbDurks collapse and is safe.

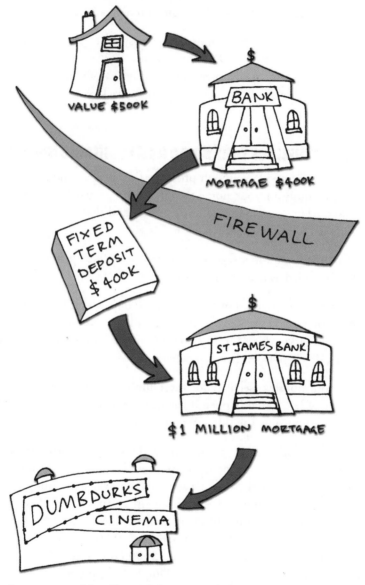

   The investor would still owe the original $400,000 mortgage on their home (which was raised to put the funds into the fixed deposit), but their home and this mortgage would be clear and unhindered by the DumbDurks disaster.

This is a much smarter strategy than mortgaging your home (and therefore exposing it to potential risk) so that you can finance a property deal. Use your assets to grow your wealth but take the advice of a good accountant (see Preferred Suppliers page at www.richmastery.com) to ensure you receive maximum protection by using intelligent asset protection structures.

Remember, smart investors use smart advisers.

Step #6 ... Insure Your Future Income

Apart from insuring against personal injury and sickness, what this rule is all about is making sure your money works for you. It's about putting your money out to work, and buying your toys from what your money earns.

Investing lets you enjoy your money many times over. You see, if you are spending all you earn, what's left over? Nothing. If you were to invest what you earn and spend what your investments produce, you could spend forever because it would be producing a never-ending income stream.

The reality is you may have to go without for a few years until your investments reach critical mass, but it will happen if you persevere.

Put your money to work first, and then spend what it makes.

Step #7 ... Increase Your Earning Potential

Just because a job pays well, it doesn't mean it'll make you rich. Work to LEARN, not just to earn.

The only reason to work is to LEARN, not to EARN. Except if you have an unusually high salary, that is.

Work trades TIME for MONEY; there is no leverage and as soon as you stop trading TIME, the MONEY stops also. Investing is about creating true wealth that includes a passive income stream (MONEY) so that you can spend your TIME doing whatever you like because the MONEY just keeps on rolling in!

▌ Six Ways To Become Rich

> What's money? A man is a success if he gets up in the morning and goes to bed at night and in between does what he wants to do.
>
> *Bob Dylan*

There are only six ways to become rich. Which one you choose all depends on you, your circumstances and your motivation. I'm not suggesting that one is better than the others, but I have my preferences. Some ways are more likely to produce my desired results than others.

The six ways are:

- Win money.
- Marry into money.
- Become a superstar.
- Invest in property.
- Invest in business.
- Invest in the stock market

I know many people who have become rich using each of these methods. They all work, and they can all get you there. It's just I don't fancy my chances as a Superstar too much. I'm not bad with the football, and there are worse voices around than mine. But if I were banking on them making me a fortune, I'll probably sadly disappoint my family and myself. The upside is I'll save them the embarrassment, that's for certain.

 Understand this: Income comes from only four sources; *taxes, donations, people at work, or your money at work.*

Let's probe this a little deeper. If you decided to make your fortune through working, how much do you think you could make? What would your limit be?

What do you have to do then, to get it rolling?

31

It's all about getting the ball rolling. The hard part is being able to accumulate that first bit of money to get the investment ball rolling.

The first thing is to THINK RICH. You do this by first dispelling the myths about wealth. What are these myths?

Here are four of the most popular, and they're easy to debunk.

1. Only LUCKY people are rich.
2. Only TALENTED people are rich.
3. There are NO MORE OPPORTUNITIES left.
4. You have to SCORE BIG.

Unless you got your wealth from winning the lottery, there's no luck involved with becoming rich. You must realize we are all talented. We all have some unique talents we should harness to our benefit.

When you look for opportunities, you will find them. If you aren't looking, you won't recognize the world's best deal if you tripped over it. And believe me when I say great opportunities present themselves every single day.

You certainly don't have to score big to become wealthy. Most rich people just accumulate wealth regularly and relentlessly. Even if it is on a small scale, it can produce great wealth if it is accumulated regularly over a long period of time.

If you were to look at the basic characteristics of the average millionaire, you'd find they are just ordinary people. The basic message I want you to understand is this; BE rich, don't ACT rich.

If you were to walk down your average neighbourhood street, you'd probably pass one or two millionaires and not know it. You see, they are no different from anyone else. They are just ordinary people.

What Stops You From Investing?

What is it that prevents 95% of the population from investing? Why is it that, even though most understand the need to invest, they just don't seem to be able to do anything about it until it's too late?

If you could understand the reasons, then do you think you'd be able to do something about it? Do you think you'd have a good chance of ensuring you don't belong to that 95% when it comes time for you to retire? You bet!

If I were to tell you there are eight primary factors that stop you from investing, do you think you could do something about it?

Good. Here are those eight factors:

1. Habit

We do what we do because of well-ingrained habits. A habit is something we do automatically. But habits can be changed. It only takes 21 days to instil a new habit, that's all. Just concentrate on doing something in a different manner for 21 days and it will become a habit. Or concentrate on not doing something for 21 days and you'll lose the habit. Remember, a break-through usually follows a break-with, a break-apart, a break-up, or a break-down. Sometimes we need one of these things to happen before we can make a break-through in changing a habit. Always replace a habit with one that is more beneficial to you. This is what I like to call a RICHual.

2. Tradition

What you've always done in the past won't solve the problems of the future. Past thoughts and actions may have been effective then, but they'll probably not be effective in meeting the demands of the future. If you want things to change in your life, YOU have to change. It's that simple. Remember, if you choose not to change, you will keep getting the same results as you're currently getting.

3. Peer pressure

How many times have you made a decision based on what other people thought? What your family or friends thought? Understand this: if you allow other people to make your decisions, you'll get the results that 95% of the population would get. Either change the people you associate with, or remember this: what other people think of me is none of my business.

4. Lack of knowledge

Keep learning every day, because if you think education is expensive, try IGNORANCE. Learning is a four-step process. Once you see it this way, it becomes easier. Here they are:

1. *Unconscious incompetence:* This is when you don't even know that you don't know something. We've all been there. How would you know you need to learn about a particular aspect of investing, if you weren't aware it existed?

2. *Conscious incompetence:* As you experience things, you become aware you're lacking in knowledge in a certain field. At least you now have the choice to do something about it.

3. *Conscious competence:* Now you can do it, but you have to be totally focused on it. Remember the first time you drove a car or rode a bike?

4. Unconscious competence: Once you have mastered something, you can do it without thinking. Like driving a car. Once you're experienced, you can listen to the radio or engage in conversation while driving. You're able to co-ordinate the gears, clutch and steering without consciously giving it any thought.

When I first learnt the four steps of learning, I believed I had to go back three steps to conscious incompetence to learn a new way of doing something. I found this extremely difficult, as my natural instinct was to go forward, not backward. Now I understand the stairs just keep going and I have to continue to learn even though I believe I may understand all there is to learn. There is so much out there that we don't even know that we don't know.

5. Fear

If you allow fear to stop you from investing, you are leading a second-class life. What I mean by this is you are consciously making a decision that results in your lifestyle and enjoyment being limited because you are allowing a negative emotion to operate your life. You may not be in control of your destiny. However, you are in charge of the decisions you make on your journey. By understanding what fear really is, you'll see how you have been deceived. Fear stands for **F**alse **E**xpectations **A**ppearing **R**eal. Fear is nothing more than an illusion. Illusions are easily dealt with. However, one of the results of fear is stress.

> **Remember this: if you have no influence over it, you shouldn't concern yourself with it.** We all have concerns. Concerns with our health, work, international affairs, the environment, the economy or today's youth. Some of these things we can do something about and some we can't. If we spend most of our effort worrying about things we can't influence, we will tend to lead reactive lives.

However, there will be some things within what I call our 'Circle of Concern' that we can influence. Perhaps our work and our health are areas where we do have some influence. These then fall within our Circle of Influence. If we were to focus on the things we can influence, we would lead a more proactive life. The trick is to slowly expand our Circle of Influence to include some of the things that were previously only of concern to us. If we can do this, we will grow.

So, how can we cope with stress? If you're feeling rather stressed, ask yourself two questions; on a scale of 1 to 10, how life threatening is it? And, am I doing the best I can? If so, just keep doing the best you can at that time. You'll realize that, until now, you have always coped, so why wouldn't you in the future? Just get stuck in and do what you have to do.

6. Apathy

Apathy can be a very strong reason stopping you from investing. To understand apathy, let's consider what it is that motivates us. There are three main motivators; fear, desire and greed. Fear is a very popular motivator. People may have a fear of being unable to finance their retirement, a fear of failure or even a fear of death. Of course, we all know that greed motivates many, but that's a negative motivator because it often blinds you to the real issues or risks. Greed is really only fear in disguise, a fear of being without. We all desire things, and if we desire them enough, we can become focused on achieving them. We become stirred into *ACTION*.

To overcome your apathy to investing, you need to change your behaviour or thought processes. You need to take a conscious decision to invest. Here's my formula for change:

$$D \times V + F > R$$

This means **Dis-satisfaction**, multiplied by **Vision**, plus the **First Steps** have to be greater than your **Resistance**.

Six ways to become rich

If you want to change you need to increase your level of dissatisfaction or you need someone to help you increase your vision. You also need someone to help you take your first steps, or to reduce your resistance.

Some people teach that you have to hit rock bottom before you are able to change. That's stupidity. I'd much rather have less resistance to change because then things don't have to get too bad before I make the decision. You see, to change what you're doing doesn't mean you first have to stop what you're doing.

Most people give something a go, then, if it doesn't work, they simply give up and focus their attention on reinventing the wheel. They try to develop a system from scratch, instead of fine-tuning their original attempt and trying again. They should try a different approach until it works.

> To change something in your own life, you don't need to be totally dissatisfied. You do need a vision, some guidance and, most importantly, you need to overcome your resistance to change. You need to change your thought process.

1. Pride

Some people would rather LOOK rich than BE rich. Consider these scenarios. A person bought his first house for $100,000 and started repaying his loan at $600 a month. After three years he sold for $120,000, paid off a few debts and bought a bigger house for $150,000 with a loan repayment of $900 a month. Then three years later, he again wanted to upgrade, so he sold for $180,000, paid off his car and bought another house for $200,000. The loan repayments went up to $1,200 a month. Three years later he was tempted with an offer on his house of $250,000, so he sold, thinking he had done extremely well, having basically upgraded from a $100,000 house to one worth $250,000 in nine years. In reality, he still owed about $200,000 to the bank, but he did have $50,000 in cash.

Sound familiar? Yes, I'm sure it does. We've all done it.

But if that same person had focused on wealth creation right from the start, from the time he bought his first house, he would have hung on to the house and swallowed his pride, increasing his repayments to $900 a month after three years, then $1,200 a month after six. After nine years he would have paid the house off, and it would probably have doubled in value. So he would be worth at least $200,000 without owing anything.

In the first scenario, our imaginary friend would be LOOKING rich with his $250,000 house, but the person in the second scenario would BE rich with a $200,000 house that he owes nothing on, and $50,000 in the bank.

2. Identity

How do you see yourself? Do you think of yourself as being RICH, an Investor, Wealthy, Smart, and Successful? This is most important.

You see, your greatest asset is your mind.

You need to think about the characteristics that identify you as an investor. They could include integrity, passion, honour, creativity, open-mindedness, decisiveness, discipline, risk-taking ability, adaptability, motivation, focus, confidence, persistence, knowledge and being proactive.

Can this become your identity? Why not? There's no reason at all why it shouldn't. You see, it's a simple matter of making your mind up that it will. Just be clear about the results you want to achieve. You might have to change a few things, like worrying about what other people think about you. The decision's yours. It can be done.

Right now, jot down all the things you think you are. Then, take a clean sheet of paper and write down all the things you need to do to give you the identity of a property investor. That's right – draw up an Identity Profile of the person you want to become.

 Remember this: the two most powerful words in the English language when put together are 'I am'.

How will this look? What sort of personality traits will you need to succeed as a property investor?

The typical characteristics you might write down could include the following:

- I am creative
- I am competent
- I am knowledgeable
- I am motivated
- I am always learning
- I am committed
- I am decisive
- I am organised

- I am forward thinking
- I am positive
- I am a good negotiator
- I am healthy
- I am honest
- I am a great investor
- I am a rich thinker

Once you have compiled your list, revisit it regularly to remind yourself who you choose to become. And be prepared for people to get in the way and distract you. If this happens, move away. Only associate with positive, like-minded people. The fact of the matter is that unless you focus on achieving this, you'll slide back into the person you were. That means you'll achieve the results you were achieving. You need to constantly grow towards the person you want to become. It's much the same for a tree – it either grows or dies.

The important thing to realise is that it's not what changes in the market place that's going to determine whether you become a successful Real Estate investor. It's not changes in the economy or your financial situation, but the changes that take place inside your head. Your level of knowledge and your thought processes is what makes all the difference. I like to put it this way – it's what you're saying to yourself, about yourself, when you're by yourself, that affects yourself most. This is the only thing that, at the end of the day, is going to affect how rich you become. Have the right attitude, and you'll create the right life for yourself. It's really as simple as that. Anyone can do it – it's just a matter of whether they choose to or not. Understand that everyone wants to *have* things; some people understand they need to *do* something in order to have what they want. Very few people understand they need to *be* the person who can *do* what is required, to *have* whatever they need in life. In other words you are a human being, NOT a human doing or a human having, so work on YOU. Be the best you that you can be.

What Keeps You Investing?

There are only really two things that keep a person investing. They are RESOLVE and COMMITMENT. And if you think about it carefully, both of these qualities require DISCIPLINE.

Investing is like anything else that takes time. You need to keep at it to reap the rewards. But, like anything else, it's easy to give up prematurely. It's easy to fall by the wayside. It's easy to tell yourself it's all too hard. It's easy to tell yourself to take a break for a while.

When it comes to investing, you MUST choose one of the two types of PAIN ... DISCIPLINE or REGRET. It's no different from life in general, if you think about it.

Think of it this way. The pain of discipline is like the pain you get when stubbing your toe. It hurts for a little while, but you know it will end soon.

If you don't choose the pain of discipline, you MUST live with the pain of regret. This pain is like the pain of cancer – it takes a major operation and extensive treatment to cure it.

Discipline is the more important option. I'd rather have the small pain of discipline than the huge pain of regret later on.

Now consider what Nelson Mandela said in his inaugural speech:

Our deepest fear is not that we are inadequate.
Our deepest fear is that we are powerful beyond measure.
It is our light, not our darkness that frightens us.
We ask ourselves, "Who am I to be brilliant?"
Actually, who are you NOT to be?
You are a child of God.
Your playing small doesn't serve the world.
There's nothing enlightened about shrinking
So that other people won't feel insecure around you.
We were born to make manifest the Glory of God that is within us.
It is not just in some of us; it's in everyone.
And as we let our own light shine,
We unconsciously give other people the permission to do the same.
As we are liberated from our own fear,
Our presence automatically liberates others.

You were born to be the best person you possibly can be. You don't have a right not to be. Then, when you achieve the goals you set yourself, it's important to reward yourself. Every time you achieve a goal, give yourself a reward. Of course, you do need to be realistic here, but every human being needs both recognition and reward. The best form of recognition you can receive is self-recognition. The same goes for rewards. Take the time to give yourself rewards. This is the surest way to achieving continual success. If you don't do this, you may not get very far at all.

Six ways to become rich

OK, so now you've a very good idea of the person you need to become to succeed in Real Estate. You see yourself as this new person. You can even feel yourself being rich.

Your mind might be right, but the stark reality is you're up to your eyeballs in debt. What can you do about it so you can get on and live the life of a rich Real Estate investor?

You need to get out of debt.

■ Getting out of debt

Debt is the prolific mother of folly and of crime.

Benjamin, Earl of Beaconsfield Disraeli
(1804–1881)

Getting out of debt has to be one of the most important, and difficult, tasks facing the average family today. With such easy credit available, it's no wonder the average family is sinking deeper and deeper into debt.

But understand this: there is good debt and bad. Sometimes it is necessary to incur debt to move forward. Sometimes you could do a whole lot better than living totally debt-free. By utilizing the equity you have in your home, for instance.

But if you're like most people, you probably have more debt than you're comfortable with. So what can you do to reduce it? Forget about refinancing, as this will merely prolong the agony by spreading out what you owe over a longer period and, usually, at a far greater real cost to you at the end of the day.

Here's what I suggest.

Firstly, sit down and take stock. Make a list of all the debts you have. Don't worry about items like food, insurance premiums or transport costs such as fuel or train fares. What I'm talking about is all your consumer debt.

Then write down next to each item your monthly repayments for each. Now divide the repayment into the amount of the debt to arrive at a ratio. This is a simple ratio that doesn't take factors like time or interest rates into account. They're not important for this exercise and need not confuse the issue. Keep it simple.

Let's assume the table you drew up looks like this. And by the way, this is a real life example of a young couple I coached many years ago.

Getting out of debt

	Loan Total	Monthly's	Ratio
House	$100,000	$1,000	100
Car 1	$17,000	$600	29
Car 2	$9,000	$350	26
Mastercard	$4,500	$250	18
Visa	$6,000	$300	20
Store Card	$1,500	$100	15
P/Loan	$8,000	$300	27
Totals	$146,000	$2,900	

Now we also need to consider your family's income. Let's assume you are a two-income family, as this couple was.

Monthly Income #1	$3,600 after tax
Monthly Income #2	$1,500 after tax
Total Monthly Income:	$5,100
Monthly Repayments:	$2,900
Total less monthly Repayments:	$2,200
Less another 10% of Monthly's:	$2200-$290
That leaves:	$1,910 to live on.

Now, this brings us to the exciting part ... getting rid of your debts. Or putting it more positively, taking control of your financial situation. Here's what you do:

Step 1

Start by focusing on the debt with the lowest ratio first. In our example, that's the Store Card. Then take the $290 you've set aside above and add it to the regular amount you pay into your Store Card. That's the extra 10% from your net amount left over after setting aside enough to pay off your usual monthly repayments. You'll notice that your regular debt repayments will, from now on, be $3,190. That's $2900 + $290.

Step 2

Once you've repaid the Store Card, tackle the debt with the next lowest ratio. In our example, it's the Mastercard. This time you'll be able to increase your normal Mastercard repayment of $250 by $390. Get it? You see, you will now no longer be paying off your Store Card, so you can add the $390 ($100 regular repayment + $290 additional payment) that you were paying towards it to your Mastercard repayment. Now by repaying this debt by $640 instead of $250 each month, you'll pay it off very much quicker.

Step 3

Continue as above until all your debts are repaid. Using the above example, it would take you four years nine months to clear the debt. Impossible? Work it out – you'll be pleasantly surprised. But let me help you. The first debt, the Store Card, will be paid off in four months. Then adding these payments to that of the Mastercard, this will be paid off in ten months. Next is the Visa card, which will be settled in 14 months, the 2nd car in 18 months, the personal loan in 21 months, the 1st car in 25 months and the house in 57 months. Understand this: that's 57 months from the time you started aggressively getting rid of your debt, not 57 months after you paid off your 1st car. Your entire debt problem will be a thing of the past in just four years and nine months. How quick is that?

What does it take to do this? What does it take to stick to a plan like this? It's very simple. All you have to do is to STOP SPENDING. Make sure you only buy what is absolutely necessary. Avoid the temptation of buying unnecessarily on your credit card or other charge cards. Postpone buying that new car you always wanted. Run you existing car for a year or two longer. Suddenly you'll find you're out of the woods.

You'll now probably wonder whether you should keep going with the plan until your house is paid off. Of course, it's not easy to give a definitive answer to that question because your own individual plans might be different from mine. Your timeframe could also be quite different.

But as a general rule, I'd say find out what your house is worth, borrow the equity you have in it and re-invest in another property. However, you might really want to pay your home off as soon as possible. In that case, increase the repayments as you've done with your other debts and continue until you own it outright. Then just think of the borrowing power you'd enjoy. You'd be able to put up a significant investment (your paid off house) as security. With that sort of start, you'll be well on your way to becoming wealthy. And it will all be because you had developed the discipline to control your spending earlier on.

Budgeting

You may be asking yourself where the extra $290 came from in our example in the first place. You might be shaking your head and saying that if it were you, you'd be most unlikely to be able to trim your regular expenses to provide the extra 10% necessary to begin the journey on the road to becoming debt-free.

The truth of the matter is it's all about budgeting. The challenge you face is developing a DAILY budget. You see, having a weekly or even monthly budget is all very well, but when you're trying to MAXIMIZE your spending power and MINIMIZE any surprises, the vagaries of weekly or monthly cycles just aren't accurate enough. That's because some months have four weeks while others have five. Some accounts are only due monthly, whereas others are payable quarterly. Ensuring these don't catch you short requires DAILY budgeting. That way you will avoid being fooled into thinking you have extra money left over in a particular week, when in fact the surplus should be accumulating to pay a quarterly bill later on. So many people are tempted into spending a weekly surplus instead of putting it aside for an upcoming bill.

You should also consider re-arranging some of your known payments like car insurance premiums and services. I come across people all the time who get caught out when buying a new car. At the time of purchase, they also take out comprehensive insurance on the car, and, when it's time to pay the second insurance payment a year later, guess what? They discover the car is also due for registration and a major service. That's three hefty payments in one month. A bit of foresight and careful planning can ensure these payments are spread.

If becoming debt-free is so easy, then why don't more people do it? That's a very good question. You see, there's really no need for poverty in this day and age. There's no reason for anyone not being able to pay his or her bills. Most people simply don't understand how to manage their money properly. If you were to take your expenses and express them as a percentage of your income, when your income varies, provided you maintain the percentages, your budget will always balance.

Why We Invest In Real Estate.

It all comes down to where we can get the best rate of return for our money over the long-term. And if you consulted ten experts or advisers, you'd probably get ten different answers. Many of the answers will be subjective, and many will be because people have vested interests. This is just a fact of life.

There are several different investment philosophies and we believe you need to understand them before you can begin to understand why we have chosen to invest as we do.

Firstly, there are those who believe you only need to provide for your retirement instead of looking to the government to look after this for you. This group buys a property, pays it off as quickly as they can and then buys the next one. They would normally only acquire about 4 or 5 properties in their lifetime. Now this is OK if all you want to do is substitute the pension with your own investment income, but you will also need to replace the benefits you would have received from the pension.

The second philosophy is to buy property for the income it produces. The purchaser owns the property, so they can receive the income produced by the tenants. Lease purchase and vendor financed deposits (I'll explain all these later) all come under this category. This is great if all you need is cashflow, but most of us need to accumulate high growth assets (like equity through capital growth) as well. Most positive cashflow properties deliver great cashflow but regularly these properties are not located in High Capital Growth areas.

The third philosophy is to buy property for its asset value without worrying about the rental returns. This is normally known as negative gearing. This will achieve great Capital Growth and, in time, reasonable rental income, but it's totally dependent on your ability to service the debt from your own income sources. In these days of uncertainty, we believe it to be unwise to commit your entire retirement future to this strategy.

So let me tell you why I invest in Real Estate and then we'll get into our strategies.

I believe the attributes of a good investment include capital growth, security, tax advantages, income, and I need to be in charge of the decisions. It must also be readily cashed.

Let's consider how the various investment options stack up against these criteria.

CAPITAL GROWTH

- Cash performs badly here, as there are no capital growth prospects.
- Stocks, on the other hand, fare better in the longer term, averaging about 5.9% compound per annum in Australia over the last 100 years (Standard & Poor's Australian Stock Price Movements One Hundred Year History).
- In most countries like Australia and New Zealand, we are of the opinion that property has averaged around 11% compound per annum over the last 100 years.

SECURITY

- If it's security you're after, then cash is for you. It is a very safe option.
- When it comes to stocks, the banks will usually accept 25% to 50% of face value as security.
- Property fares best in the security stakes, with banks mostly willing to accept over 90% of a property's value as security.

TAX ADVANTAGES

- There are no tax advantages associated with cash. In fact, it's quite the opposite. You are taxed on the interest you earn from cash investments.
- Stocks, dividend imputation and negative gearing can and do offer some very good tax relief.
- Property, on the other hand, offers the investor excellent tax advantages. Paper losses associated with depreciation are totally tax deductible.

INCOME

- Cash does produce a reliable income stream. However, it is small in percentage terms. It is also easily eroded by inflation.
- Stocks don't produce a reliable income stream because dividends are dependent upon the company's performance and whether a profit was made or not.

- Property performs well on this score. Tenants provide a steady, reliable source of indexed income. Even low occupancy rates are not a challenge, provided you understand the market.

CONTROL

- The only control you have with cash is which bank you deposit it in.
- With stocks, control rests with company directors and fund managers. All you can do is decide which stocks to buy, when to buy and when to sell.
- Property offers the investor complete, and insurable, control.

READILY CASHED

- This is one of cash's traditional strong points. With the exception of cash tied up in term deposits, it is very easy to get your hands on it if you need to.
- Stocks, too, are easily cashed in - just give your broker an instruction to sell, and within a day or so you will have the proceeds deposited into your nominated bank account. The challenge lies, of course, with the state of the market at the time you sell. Market volatility affects the stock price.
- Property is generally more difficult to convert into cash. It takes time. However, you can borrow against the property if you are in desperate need of cash provided you have maintained a correct balance in your portfolio.

OK, let's now consider an example to illustrate why we prefer investing in Real Estate.

Let's assume you have $150,000 that you want to invest. Suppose you were to deposit this in a bank account. Let's also suppose it was your lucky day and you locked the money up at an interest rate of 7%.

INVESTMENT	= $150,000
INTEREST EARNED	= 7%
INCOME	= $10,500

Now let's assume you are on an income tax rate of 48.5%, this is similar to the top tax rate for many countries like Australia and the US.

TAX PAYABLE	= $5,092
NET INCOME	= $5,408
NET RETURN	= 3.6%
Or, put another way ... 7% less 48.5% tax	= 3.6%

This isn't the end of the story. Let's now assume INFLATION to be running at 3%. Our net return after inflation is therefore only 0.6%.

That's a 0.6% return after tax and inflation.

Using the **Rule of 72** (see the Appendix for further details), it would take 120 years to double your money. I'd rather double it every year or two. And through investing in Real Estate, you can.

So let's now look at how you'd fare if you took that same $150,000 and bought a property instead of putting it in the bank. Again, for the sake of comparison, we will make a few basic assumptions. Let's assume the $150,000 property represents fair value. Let's also assume this property returns a very conservative rental income of $150 a week. How do the figures now look?

INVESTMENT	= $150,000
INCOME (Rent of $150 per week)	= $7,500

Now let's again assume you are on an income tax rate of 48.5% (Similar to the top tax rate for Australia and the US).

TAX RATE (assume no deductions)	= $3,637
NET INCOME	= $3,863

Now we need to make another very conservative assumption, this time on the rate of capital growth.

CAPITAL GROWTH (8%)	= $12,000
TOTAL NET INCOME	= $15,863

If we were to now look at our after tax return on equity, we get a very respectable 10.575%.

Remember, a stock broker will show you this as a 5% yield (the $7,500 rental return divided by the $150,000 property price). This is not correct as it assumes there is no capital growth.

I'm never interested in the yield of a property because I never pay cash for it in the first place. It's the stupidest thing to do. If you own your own home outright, please reconsider your thinking, as it amounts to throwing your biggest asset away in the rubbish bin. The major advantage Real Estate has over other investment strategies is the ability to leverage a small amount of capital into a large investment.

Again, let's see how the figures would pan out if you took the same $150,000 and bought a house, at fair value, but this time leveraged with 85% finance. Let's assume you secured the loan at a high interest rate of 9%, and that, once again, you were to receive 7% yield or only able to get $150 a week in rent from a tenant.

DEPOSIT	= $22,500
BORROW	= $127,500
INTEREST PAID (9%)	= $11,475
INCOME (Rent $150 per week)	= $7,500
PRE-TAX Negative Cashflow	= -$3,975
TAX REBATE (assume no other deductions)	= $1,928
CASH CONTRIBUTION NEEDED	= $2,047
CAPITAL GROWTH (8%)	= $12,000
NET TOTAL RETURN	= $9,953

To calculate your after tax return on equity, you work this out on your capital invested, which in this case is your deposit.

AFTER TAX RETURN ON EQUITY	= 44.23%

Now let's consider what would happen if you were to go the whole hog and borrow the lot to buy this $150,000 house.

DEPOSIT	= $0
BORROW	= $150,000
INTEREST PAID (9%)	= $13,500
INCOME (Rent $150 per week)	= $7,500
PRE-TAX Negative Cashflow	= -$6,000
Tax Rebate (48.5%) (assume no other deductions)	= $2,910
CASH CONTRIBUTION NEEDED	= $3,090
CAPITAL GROWTH (8%)	= $12,000
NET TOTAL RETURN	= $8,910

In this case, to calculate your after tax return on equity, you'd compare your net total return with the total amount of cash you contributed.

AFTER TAX RETURN ON EQUITY	= 288.35%

Note: The depreciation and tax rates used are solely to illustrate this example. The investment principles taught in this example are universally applicable in every country in the world.

The challenge here is that you're getting this fabulous rate of return on the small amount of money you contributed during the year. But as part of a balanced portfolio, this will work exceptionally well. We don't like negative gearing generally but if we must, we set up a property to give us this sort of return as part of our portfolio. We'll be quite happy to do it, as long as it's not us that's contributing to the loss on the property. You need to be clear on why you want to negatively gear a property in the first place. Many people choose this option simply for the tax advantages and not the profit it will produce. Don't buy property to make a loss to reduce your tax; the profit should be on the property.

Stocks vs. Property

If we were to compare stocks with property as an investment medium, what would we find? Well, to be quite honest, I couldn't find very much. Let me explain…

I thought I'd compare the top 100 stocks with the top 100 properties and found it was like comparing apples (stocks) with oranges (properties). What I found was they kept replacing bad apples with good ones on the stock market. This means you are always comparing the best 100 apples they can find, whereas with Real Estate, they don't do that. I could not get statistics for the top 100 stocks from 100 years ago. There are no records of which ones made the indices back then. Property, on the other hand, is tangible – it's always there. The records are accessible and easily understandable. However, the Real Estate Institute of Australia doesn't keep median prices for Australia as a whole. This makes general comparisons difficult.

Most people understand only two basic philosophies for investing in Real Estate. You buy a property for the cashflow it will give you, or you buy a property for the capital growth it will give you.

The same two philosophies apply to the stock market. Many people who invest in stocks in a big way do very well and are quite happy with their strategy.

But consider this: I believe Real Estate is up to 20 times more effective than stocks as an investment strategy for all the reasons I'm about to list, and more. The reality is that many companies on the stock market invest their surplus capital in Real Estate. They buy property. They deduct all the expenses they can first, and then, as a shareholder, you get what's left. Check the fine print in company quarterly and annual reports – you will be amazed what you find.

It's also a sad reality that many companies become takeover targets just for their Real Estate worth. And it's also a sad reality that with stocks, the only time you make a profit is when someone else makes a loss. To really succeed on the stock market, you need to dedicate yourself to learning all aspects of fundamental and technical analysis, keep in touch with a professional team, monitor the market constantly and trade full-time if possible. It's a whole lot harder than watching your money grow in Real Estate while you sleep.

Value and Price

Another reason I invest in Real Estate is the difference between value and price. What do I mean by this? Let me explain…

Who determines a property's price? The buyer, every time.

Understand this: sellers always think in terms of value when deciding what price they will list their property at. They take into account things like location, features, the quality of fittings used during the last makeover or renovation, the swimming pool, and the fact that theirs has electric garage doors instead of manual ones. Buyers, on the other hand, think only in terms of price. They have a budget and a figure the bank has approved. And they want to bargain. It's the buyers who call the shots because they have the cash. This is the reality of the situation. Just because a property might be listed at market value, it doesn't mean the seller won't take less for it. They might have really good reasons why they must sell there and then.

So remember, because Real Estate is an illiquid market (that is it's not readily converted into cash), the buyer usually determines the sale price. Whereas with stocks, the price is the price on that day. With Real Estate, smart investors always get a discount.

The Number Of Zeros

Another reason I choose to invest in Real Estate is what I call the 'number of zeros' factor. You see, selling a $2.00 hamburger can make you rich – but you've got to sell millions of them. In property, the average deal will make you tens of thousands of dollars, and this is a year's wage for some. A good deal can make you hundreds of thousands of dollars or even millions.

Let's look at this a little closer.

Suppose you want to make $500,000 a year from property and not just $50,000. How do you go about it?

If you're buying properties worth $50,000 and aim to make 10% on each deal, you make $5,000 on each. If you do a deal a month, you'll be making $60,000 a year. Now for some, that's reasonable. If you want to be doing a whole lot better, you've just got to add a zero to the figures. You see, if you started dealing in properties that cost $500,000 and not $50,000, you'd then make $50,000 a month on a 10% margin, or $600,000 a year.

So, what's stopping you from adding a zero?

Generally it's FEAR. People are often scared of a debt of this magnitude.

> **Understand this:** if you go broke for $50,000 or for $500,000, you're still broke. The only difference is it's really a crime to go broke for just $50,000. If you owe $5,000 to the bank you have a problem, but if you owe $50,000,000 to the bank, they have a problem. If you owed $50,000,000, the bank wouldn't let you go broke that easily. They would have advisers working out how to save you from bankruptcy.

We've been brought up to believe it's wrong to owe money. It's good to owe money as long as it's good debt, not bad.

With property, it's just the number of zeros you're prepared to work with that will determine your end result. Understand that it's easier to work on $500,000 deals than $50,000 deals. There is a lot less competition with hardly anyone playing at that level. You need to think BIG to win BIG. You're still playing the same game but at a higher level; it's just that a few rules are slightly different and you might have to be a bit more careful. But you do have more room for error. You see, if you're dealing with a cheaper property and you only have a $10,000 margin of error, that can get swallowed up pretty quickly. But if you're talking about a million-dollar property, you have many more numbers to play with, even though the error margin might be the same in percentage terms.

Added Value

Another reason I like investing in Real Restate is because I can easily add value to the property. With Real Estate, you can add value quickly and easily by tidying the garden, doing a splash of painting, building a carport, erecting a fence, or installing a new dryer and dishwasher.

For every $10 extra you get for weekly rent you usually add an extra $5,200 to the valuation of your property ($10 a week for 52 weeks is an additional $520 a year, and when capitalised at 10%, that equates to an increase in valuation of $5,200).

Adding value to my investments is what I'm after. If I buy a property for $50,000, spend $1,500 on it to increase it's worth to (let's say) $55,000, I can refinance it and recover all my money. I then have a property that pays for itself yet I have no money tied up in it. It's all very simple. You've just got to understand what to do to add value to a property. You need to understand where to spend money and where not to spend. We'll go into the details soon.

Getting Into Debt

I mentioned getting into debt earlier on. Getting into debt isn't always a bad thing. Of course, it makes a huge difference whether the debt you're about to take on is good debt or bad debt. There's a big difference between these two. Let me explain.

Good debt is that which makes you money. It's used to buy assets. It's something someone else pays for on your behalf. Bad debt, on the other hand, is something YOU have to pay for. It's consumer debt. You pay for it with your after-tax money. Unfortunately, this is the type of debt most people accumulate.

Let's consider a few examples. Cars can be good debt. But things like cameras, computers, VCRs and other toys are bad debt. I'll never ever owe money on them. You see, the day you buy them, they're worth nothing. Technology is already obsolete the day you buy. And if you sold it a week after you bought, you'd only get back a fraction of the price you paid.

But with Real Estate it's different. The banks are lining up to provide you and I with money to buy good properties. But that doesn't mean they hand out the folding stuff to anyone. There are certain criteria they look at. You still do need to satisfy certain requirements. To put it simply, there are three attributes you'll need if you want to borrow money. They are:

- Strength of income
- Strength of assets
- Strong nerves

When you are considering borrowing, just remember valuations are one thing, but serviceability is still a bank's main concern. Their bottom-line is ensuring they minimise their risks.

It's not so much about how much you can borrow; it's rather about how much you can service that's important here.

Leverage

Leverage is another reason we invest in Real Estate. It's a simple concept but a very effective one. It's all about doing more with less. If you have $10,000 in cash, you can buy property in a price range between $50,000 and $100,000.

 Understand that $100,000 going up by 10% gives you a $10,000 return. So if you only have $10,000 invested, that's a 100% return.

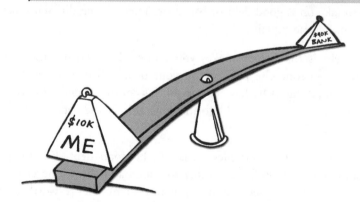

Property is only ever a good investment if it's leveraged. If it isn't, it's pretty ordinary. You see, a business will provide you with much higher rates of returns than property will, but how much can you borrow against a business? You'd be doing very well indeed if you could borrow 60% of your stock value.

Rental Income

Rental income is a great reason for investing in Real Estate. Consider that even though $5,000 a year in rental income on a $100,000 property is only a 5% yield, that doesn't worry me. You see, I love tenants because they pay off the property for me. Just as McDonalds uses the Big Mac to pay for its buildings, I use tenants to pay for a percentage of the property's expenses while I collect the capital growth.

Tax Deductions

Tax deductions make investing in Real Estate a very attractive option. The government can't afford to provide housing for everyone, so they give you and I a tax deduction as an additional incentive to provide it for them.

When you purchase a property, you are buying an asset made up of a number of items that are all wearing out over time and will eventually need repairing or replacing. The land of course is the exception to this. The government allows you to claim a number of 'paper deductions' by having your accountant write off a percentage of the value of each 'capitalised' item each year at rates prescribed by the Tax Office. These items include the building and its fixtures and fittings e.g. carpets, curtains, fences, garage doors, waste disposals, spa pools, decking and air conditioners to name just a few.

Along with depreciation you are able to deduct 100% of the tax related expenses for a property within the tax year such as rates, insurance, property manager's fees, mortgage interest payments, property seminar costs, subscriptions, building repairs, and any other expense that directly relates to your property investment.

One of the stunning things about Real Estate is that often when rental income exceeds all expenses and you get the property paying you weekly positive CASHFLOW, that also gives you a tax refund! How is this possible you ask? Here's an example…

Let's say we negotiate the purchase of a 3-bedroom house in one of the outer suburbs. The people need to sell, it's only a couple of years old and we pick it up for $90,000, and its real market value is about $122,000 based on what other houses are selling for in the area. I use equity in my own home to secure a 100% mortgage of $93,075 ($2,075 transaction costs eg stamp duty and $1,000 legal fees – Note: Stamp Duty does not apply in NEW ZEALAND) at 6.5% interest only.

I engage a quantity surveyor/chattels valuer to complete a Valuation Report where he details the original building construction cost at $45,000. Because it is 2 years old I start with a book value of $42,778 that I can start depreciating at 2.5% p.a. He also produces a book value of $17,100 for the fixtures and fittings, which can be depreciated at an average of 11.25% p.a.

The property rents for $160 a week, and here's how the numbers look:

Rental Income	$160 per week	$8,320
Mortgage Interest	6.5% Interest Only	-$6,050
Rates		-$600
Insurance		-$350
Repairs		-$300
Total Expenses		-$7,300
Positive Cashflow		**$1,020**

100% financed this property has paid us Positive Cashflow of $1,020 for year 1, and the exciting thing is it's tax-free! Heres how:

Depreciation - Building	$42,778 @ 2.5%	-$1,069
Depreciation – Fixtures & Fittings	$17,100 @ 11.25%	-$1,924
Total Income	Rent @ $160 per week	$8,320
Total Deductions (including depreciation)		-$10,293
Tax Loss		-$1,864
Tax Refund	@ 31.5% (your tax rate)	$587
After Tax Cashflow		**$1,607**

Note: The depreciation and tax rates used are solely to illustrate this example. The investment principles taught in this example are universally applicable in every country in the world.

Once we have deducted depreciation we have created a tax loss situation (on paper). If we had purchased the property in our name and we pay income tax on our salary/wages, at a top tax rate of 31.5%, we can then claim a tax refund of $587. If our top rate was 48.5%, then the tax refund would increase to $904.

The exciting thing in this example is that we bought the property at a discount ($32,000), we have received positive cashflow, a tax refund, and have not even considered what the capital growth could be. Let's assume it at just 6% and calculate our total return from this deal in the first year:

Equity gained at purchase	(less legals and stamp duty)	$29,925
Positive Cashflow		$1,020
Tax refund	@ 31.5%	$587
Equity Growth	At Capital Growth of 6%	$7,320
Total Year 1 Return	**Cash + Equity Earned**	**$38,852**

Property pays you up to 4 ways, if you buy right and structure it correctly for tax.

But don't make the mistake thousands of property investors make. Don't buy any investment property just for the tax benefits it provides. Look at the tax benefits as a welcome fringe benefit that just happens to be around at the time. Focus on the cashflow or the capital growth the property produces. Occasionally a property will provide you with both, but this is the exception rather than the rule. You see, properties that provide great cashflow usually have average to lower rates of capital growth, and those that provide capital growth usually produce average to lower cashflows. The important message here is to get into residential Real Estate for the right reasons and make sure you build a *balanced portfolio*.

Security

Security is another great reason I use for investing in Real Estate. Ever heard of the saying, safe as houses? Well, it's true. As an investment, property is about as safe as you can get. You see, you can insure almost anything to do with property. Everything from debt collection to the replacement of damaged items. And unlike stocks, a property has very little chance of ever disappearing … and even if it does, you'll still be insured.

Emotion

Divorce, separation, transfer, children, dogs, cats, death, sickness, travel … there are 101 reasons why people get attached to a home, and just as many why they want to sell.

> Whether you're buying or selling, **remember this**: you stick with the numbers, and let them deal with the emotion. Try never to let emotion get in the way of a good deal – from your point of view, that is. But be empathetic with the seller. Understand their situation and listen to their story. This is the quickest way to get them onto the emotional level.

Bear in mind the price you decide on is probably the right price. Your gut feeling is probably very close to the mark. You may need to play with the numbers to make the deal work, particularly how you negotiate the payment terms. But remember, the day you've got to start playing with the basic numbers (rent returns, renovation costs and future sale price) to make the deal work, is the day you need to walk away from it.

Shelter

Everyone needs to live somewhere. If you invest in the mid to low property price range, there will always be people wanting to rent.

We very seldom buy a $500,000 single dwelling property in a prime location for rental return. We buy properties in that price range for capital growth. If there happens to be a tenant in it, all well and good, but if there isn't, we don't care. Our income comes from properties in the mid to low price range. That's where the cashflow is. These properties are always in demand and they're always rented out. If you have a balanced property portfolio, then your lower priced properties will pay for your higher priced ones.

The only time we buy cashflow properties over $500,000 in value is when the figures look very, very good or we buy blocks or multiple income properties on one site.

Supply and Demand

Understanding supply and demand factors make life very easy. And what we like about it is that, as a property owner, I get to choose. I choose so that things suit me. Let me explain what I mean by this.

Owning rental property is a fairly predictable business. You see, people tend to get transferred or move areas at Christmas time. Furthermore, I can choose when I buy, where I buy and when and where I sell.

And you can go further still. Unlike most rental property owners, I don't operate on the basis of signing a six-month or yearly lease or rental agreement with my tenants. I work on the principle that the properties become vacant in early January each year. So in some cases the lease or rental agreement would be for nine months, in others for 22 months, depending when it was signed. I also never let a property become vacant on a Saturday, because then it would take me a day or two to get it cleaned and re-advertised, with the earliest prospect of re-letting it being the following Saturday. That way I lose a whole week's rent. If I choose to let it become vacant on the Wednesday, I can get it cleaned and re-advertised within a day or so, allowing me to rent it out that same Saturday, a day that also suits most people wanting to move. This way I only have the place unoccupied for a few days, and I've lost very little rent. It's a small detail, but when you're renting out as many properties like we are, it all adds up to many tens of thousands of dollars.

Population

Of course, this is in essence what it's all about. We are providing housing, at a profit, for the bulk of the population. And the population just keeps getting bigger. Not only that, but a higher and higher percentage of them are renting. Of course, some areas are better than others when it comes to rental demand, so do your homework. It's not difficult; it just takes some common sense and a little effort.

Statistics in Australia show for the last three decades that around 69% of the population own their own homes. Over this period the number of renters has grown from 24% to 30%. This is a global trend. Again, this is a fairly constant figure in percentage terms, but with the growth of the population, the number of rental households over this period has grown from 1,093,100 to 2,120,500. That means there has been an unbelievable demand for new rental properties. More than a million new rental properties have come onto the market over the last 20 years. The vast majority supplied by private investors like you and me!

Vacancy Rates

There will be times when you have no one in the property paying you rent. But this is manageable, workable and most important, insurable.

To help minimize this unprofitable period, keep your property in reasonable condition. It is important to understand that tenants aren't second-class citizens. They have a right to live in a decent, clean and tidy property. Just because it's a rental property, doesn't mean it has to be a slum. But if it is, you'll more than likely attract a pretty awful tenant. Just because someone chooses to rent, doesn't mean they don't want to live in a clean, safe place.

Now I'd like you to do this little exercise. Consider it part of your research. Imagine you are looking to rent a house for yourself to live in. Choose the area you would prefer and get out and have a look at what's available. What will you find? I'm sure you'll be surprised at how difficult it is to find a decent place that you'd be happy to live in. Many landlords seem to think anything will do.

It's not difficult to place yourself in an enviable position on the rental market just by presenting your property in a decent manner. With only a little effort and common sense, you'll have tenants clamouring after your property. By doing the right thing as a landlord, you should never have to worry about poor occupancy rates.

> If you have 1 property and it's vacant, what's your vacancy rate? 100%. If you have 10 properties and 1 is vacant, what's your vacancy rate now? 10%. If you have 100 properties and 1 is vacant, what's your vacancy rate? 1%. It amazes me that people think owning a lot of property is risky, yet the reality is the more properties you own the less risk you face financially. It's a pretty good reason for being a serious property investor who gets some runs on the board rather than someone who just dabbles with one or two properties.

Insurance

In Real Estate, everything is insurable. Well, almost everything. The only thing that isn't is a planned vacancy. But as with everything, you need to approach it with the right attitude if you want to avoid any nasty surprises.

When owning rental property, you might not need to make an insurance claim straight away. It may be that you only need to claim in a year's time for some damages suffered during the first year's tenancy. It may be only when your first tenant moves out and you are preparing the house for the next tenant that you discover something that necessitates a claim. It may be the last month of your insurance that you need to claim for fire or storm damage. Pay your premiums based on values in 12 months time. For this reason, it's better to over-insure than to under-insure. Visit the Preferred Suppliers area of www.richmastery.com and see who we recommend.

You also need to bear in mind that most insurance policies include a 'subject to average' clause. This means if you have under-insured by 50%, they will only pay out 50% of your claim. These are the rules of the game, and if you play, you must play by the rules. You must understand the rules, and if you play by them, at least you'll get paid when you make a claim. Believe me, the time will come when you will make a claim.

There are also other forms of insurance you need to consider. Most banks will insist you have mortgage insurance if you have borrowed more than 80% of the purchase price of a property. Then there's Home and Contents/Chattels insurance that is well worth taking out.

Don't take out a private household policy on a rental property. Rather take out a Landlord's policy as this generally includes some contents insurance at the base rate to cover carpets, curtains, stove, light fittings and things like that. Ensure the policy also includes property owner's liability, not just public liability – make sure you have this because if you don't, it's the sort of thing that can send you broke.

You should also consider policies that cover debt recovery, legal bills, and tenant damage. When you buy a rental property, it's important to ensure you get a landlord's protection policy or something similar. This is a very good product, as it includes checks on prospective tenants to make sure they're good tenants, checks of the tenant black list, and credit checks. If a tenant breaks a lease, lost rent is covered, and repairs up to an amount set on your policy are paid if the tenant does any damage to the property. Downtime of up to 52 weeks is also covered during the period the house is being repaired, and the cost of legal bills incurred and debt recovery costs are also included. This is a reasonable policy for the price and it guarantees your income all the time.

Another policy to consider is a Personal Accident/Sickness Income Protection policy. Your income is, after all, your greatest asset. Protect it. And don't forget to include a mortgage payout clause in your policy.

For further information on policies available, contact a reputable registered insurance broker.

Just remember to pay your premiums on time and to insure for TOO MUCH, not too little.

I have saved a packet of money by using one insurance broker to handle the insurance for all my properties and having all the policies come up for renewal at the same time. This enables the broker to negotiate a discounted bulk insurance package that saves me thousands each year. It is also a whole lot easier to have one bulk insurance renewal each year than policies coming up for renewal each week or month.

Residential Vs. Other Types Of Property

I'm often asked about the pros and cons of investing in other forms of property. Now I know many people have made good money from commercial property, but as a general rule, when you start, it is less risky if you to stick with residential property.

Let me explain why.

Commercial, Industrial, Retail and Hospitality property possess all the attributes of a good investment but involve risks beyond your control. Business managers generally become your tenants and if they do a poor job managing their businesses, they may not be able to pay the rent. Also, business downturns, changing consumer trends and all sorts of other factors could mean you don't get paid. If you own a building that has six shops, four of which are empty, what sort of interest do you think that would generate from prospective buyers, should you decide to sell?

Vacant land doesn't produce an income and has no tax benefits. If you have some spare money that you want to park somewhere, then buying a block of land is an option. But generally, we don't see it as a great investment and would prefer our invested funds deliver a tangible measurable return on our investment. Land, more often than not, does not do that.

Rural land is high risk, speculative and a lot of work. If this is what you want, then fine, but we don't recommend it.

Residential property has got to be the best option by far. You see. everyone needs shelter, and indications are that demand for rental properties is increasing all the time. One of the only residential markets we avoid is small towns that are dependent on one industry. Now that's not to say others shouldn't invest there if it appeals to them; all we're saying is they're not part of our game plan. They don't meet our rules.

Some people feel you shouldn't have all your eggs in one basket. As there are over twenty different types of residential property that we invest in – Townhouses, Apartments, Terraced Apartments, Timeshares, Purpose Built Flats, Boarding Houses, Rest Homes, Serviced Rooms, Caravan Parks, Backpacker Hostels, Granny Flats, Overnight Accommodation, Home & Income Flats, Flats above Commercial Shops, Seaside Holiday Homes, Free Standing Homes, Lifestyle Properties, Hotel Leases, Condo's, Blocks of 4, 8, 16 etc, Leasehold Titles, Strata Titles, Rural Accommodation, Bare Land (for developing) in a vast range of different cities, towns, suburbs and countries – we believe it is easy to diversify and spread the risk of your investment portfolio.

What Makes A Good Investment?

Now that you've got a pretty good idea of some of the considerations involved when deciding on how to invest, there's one other topic you need to think about. You need to decide, in your own mind, what a good investment is.

This will vary from person to person, depending on each individual's situation and the level of risk they're comfortable with. But after all the years we've been investing in Real Estate, we can't think of any more than the following:

- Capital growth
- Security
- Ability to convert into cash
- Tax advantages
- Ability to produce an income
- I'm in charge

To me, if an investment opportunity doesn't meet these criteria, it's simply speculation. We believe only residential property meets all these criteria.

Time Frame

The next thing you need to focus on is the time frame you are working with. Are your goals long-term or short-term?

In reality, a short-term investor should be known as a speculator. I don't mean to degrade short-term investments, and I do believe you need to do both kinds of deals, but you just need to keep in mind what each deal is for.

Know your goals and your outcomes, but most importantly know your timeframe.

I Playing The Game

> Money was never a big motivation for me, except as a way to keep score. The real excitement is playing the game.
>
> **Donald Trump, "Trump: Art of the Deal"**

You'll notice I refer to investing in property as 'playing the game'. If you want to enter the business of property investment, you have to abide by the rules of the game. Every game has rules, and playing the property investment game is no different.

So what then will you need to play a game? Any game.

Think about this for a minute and jot them down on a sheet of paper.

Your list will probably look something like this:

- Rules
- Playing field
- A plan
- Team
- Opposition
- Umpire or Referee
- Goals
- Scorekeeper
- Spectators
- Manager
- Coach
- Rewards
- Equipment
- Communication

OK, let's look at this a bit closer, particularly as it applies to the game of Real Estate.

Playing the game

There are in actual fact three sets of RULES you need to play by. These include:

The Rules Of The Game

These are the general rules as laid down by the Government, Local Authorities, banks, legal institutions, Real Estate agencies and local conventions. You have no control over these rules.

Your Rules Of The Game

Your overall vision, mission, goals and objectives will determine your rules. They will be established according to your overall situation and circumstances. They will reflect your *modus operandi*, ethics, morality, wishes and desires. You set these rules, and you can change them. If you do decide to change your rules, first check with a mentor or someone whose opinion you respect, to see if it is really your rules you need to change (because the environment you operate in has changed) or if it's that you are just becoming lazy or careless.

Your Specific Rules For The Specific Game You Are Playing At The Time.

These will vary according to which marketplace you are dealing in at that moment – whether you are dealing with an inner-city unit or an outer suburban refurbished house. They could also vary according to which city you are dealing in and whether you are buying a house to live in yourself or one that you are buying for capital growth only. Again, these are your rules and you can change them to suit your situation.

You could be playing many games at the same time. You could be investing in different markets. Generally speaking, there will be different rules for the following types of properties:

- Inner city units
- Inner city houses
- Fringe city units
- Fringe city houses
- Outer city units
- Outer city houses
- Satellite units (units in stand alone towns)
- Satellite houses

In addition, there are different rules governing new units, existing units and refurbished units as well as new houses, existing houses and refurbished houses.

Each market is different. The rules governing buying a new inner city unit are quite different to those that apply when buying an existing house in an outer city suburb. Then there are rules for property you intend living in yourself, property you intend renting out, property you want to buy and then sell again quickly, property you intend holding onto long-term, property you aim to get capital gain from, property you're buying for a rental purchase plan, and property you're buying through vendor finance deals. In fact there are about 27 different types of residential Real Estate categories – I like to be involved in a dozen of these at any one time.

Investing in Real Estate is like a playing a game in other respects as well. In addition to the RULES, there is the PLAYING FIELD (the market you are dealing in), your TEAM (those helping you – could be your spouse, Real Estate agent, lawyer, etc), the OPPOSITION (those who are trying to prevent you from succeeding), the UMPIRE (Government or Local Authority), the GOALS (your aims and objectives), SCORES (if you're not keeping score, why bother playing?), the LEARNING EXPERIENCE (the more you play the better you get), SPECTATORS (those who cheer you on or criticise your efforts), the SCOREKEEPERS (your accountant, bookkeeper or auditor), the RULE MAKERS (could be you, the industry or the local authority), RULE ENFORCERS (police), MANAGERS, COACHES (those who get you to achieve something you wouldn't be able to on your own), the COMPETITION (those who stimulate you to higher levels of achievement), and the TIME LIMIT (when do you stop playing the game?).

Who's Playing The Game With You?

Before you start playing the game, you need to sit down and make a list of everyone who is part of your team. You need to understand who's on your side and who's not.

Who will be helpful to have on your team? Who is essential? Make a list of all those you think you'll need.

Here's a useful list, and one that I suggest you consider:

- **Quantity Surveyor/Chattels Valuer.** This is an essential team member and one I'm never without. I send one through every property I purchase. You see, they are experts at providing a comprehensive report on every possible item I can claim a paper tax deduction on. Their report lists every item, its value and what percentage I can depreciate it at on my next tax return. They can also give you an accurate estimation of the cost of renovations that were done in the past.

- **Accountant**: The difference between a good one and a bad one can cost you thousands of dollars in lost tax deductions, and there is nothing sadder than lost tax deductions!

- **Valuer**. Use a quality valuer that is approved by your bank. Valuers assess the current market value of a property by comparing the property you are looking at with other similar house sales in the surrounding area. Many valuers or Real Estate valuation web sites offer quick estimation services for a minimal fee – they will give you an accurate guide of what the property is worth. If you think a valuer has valued a property too low, challenge them on their valuation with supporting house sales data and don't be afraid to get another valuation as a second opinion.

- **Solicitor**. The average suburban solicitor just isn't good enough if you're aiming at investing in Real Estate in a big way. You see, they are generalists. I believe you need to seek one who specialises in conveyancing (property settlement), property law and property litigation.

- **Real Estate Agent**. Do you need one on your team? And are they a good or bad thing if you're an investor? As I see it agents are a necessary evil! Many good agents that do invest in property (over 90% of them don't) will usually snap up all the good deals for themselves long before you get to hear about them. So the trick is to find a good agent who will pass you the good deals.

> Furthermore, if you were to waltz into a Real Estate office and announce you are interested in buying an investment property, many agents will show you houses with pretty gardens where the investment numbers are pathetic *(as 90% of agents don't invest in property themselves, many wouldn't know what a hot property investment looks like if they tripped over it)*. Chances are they'll start showing you stuff they've been battling to sell. Examples of these might be property that's on a main road, that has one or two major drawbacks or that needs more than a little work done to bring it up to scratch. But there's no denying you do need them.

Here's how we like to operate. To begin with, and especially when we are entering a new area, we phone three or four Real Estate agents offices to make appointments with the top agent in each office.

Why do we want the top agent, you ask? Who has negotiated more deals than anyone else in the office? Who knows the area best of all? Who is intimately in touch with the market? Who has the widest base of local contacts? Who is the best negotiator? The office's top agent, of course!

In the interview process if I come across one that impresses me, I offer to pay for a few hours of their time if they'll show me around their marketplace. They're always more than happy to do this without being paid. You see, they will gladly show me around because they know I could be the source of their next commission cheque. In fact, if they do a good job I could be the source of their next several commission cheques! But I make the offer to pay for their time nevertheless, because it shows them I'm a serious buyer who isn't wasting their time.

When the agent shows me a hot deal and the numbers look good, we enter into negotiations. If at all possible I never negotiate with the seller through the agent simply because I don't trust the agent as far as I can throw them! The reality is most of them are there only because they couldn't get another job. Most of them see themselves in transition. Now I know they're not all bad people, but most of them would rather not be doing that job. Would you want someone like that negotiating on your behalf? Especially when you know they're working for the seller? Good agents are worth their weight in gold, but they are harder to find than hen's teeth!

Now I NEVER begrudge the agent their commission. I'm always more than willing to pay them what they're due; it's just that I don't want them doing my dealing for me, if I can avoid it.

So, how do you get around that? Simple. After they've shown me the property for the first time, I return later that evening, knock on the door and say: "I was here earlier today with your agent, and I just love the place. In fact it's the best I've seen so far. We were just driving past on our way home, and my wife asked me what colour the bathroom is. I just couldn't remember, so I thought I'd stop by. Mind if I had another look?" They rarely ever refuse. And then I say I'm ready to make an offer, but I'd prefer not to go through the agent, as I didn't get on too well with them. "Of course, I'm more than willing to pay their commission, because they were the one who led me to you." Then I draw up the contract and we verbally negotiate and get it signed before I leave.

I prefer making the offer direct. What seller would run the risk of losing a sale, just because the agent wasn't the one conveying the offer to them? And in cases where I see a For Sale sign up outside a property, I've been known to go straight up, knock on the door, view the property, negotiate the deal, then drive around to the agent and hand over a cheque for their commission. You should see the surprise look on their face! In cases like that, I make an ally for life. That agent becomes part of my team and understands how I like to operate.

- **Builder & Contractors**. Get to know a good builder - a tradesman, not a hammer hand. You want a professional job done. So many people try and save a dollar by getting a cheap unqualified person who ruins the job and costs them more in the long run fixing up their mistakes. Real Estate is a long-term asset; make sure you approach all renovations or repairs to your properties with a long-term view.

Take time to understand the rules that apply here. For instance, in many countries all contractors doing building work above a certain value (eg $1,100) are required to hold a tradesperson's certificate or contractor's licence. This includes, for example, painters, tilers, structural landscapers, carpenters and builders. In most cases pest controllers, plumbers and gasfitters are all required to have certification as part of their trade. Always ask to see the tradesperson's credentials, check them out, do your due diligence.

Renovations/alterations that involve the co-ordination of several trades as part of the overall job (such as a plumber, tiler, plasterer, painter and carpenter) should only be conducted by a licensed builder. And remember, a trade contractor such as a licensed carpenter cannot conduct work that involves other trades. And one other thing: if you want to do this work yourself, be aware that you need to check first with your local building services authority to see what the rules are. In some states in Australia, for instance, if the work you want to carry out yourself comes to more than $6,600 in total, you'll need to get an owner/builder's licence. And if your renovations amount to more than $11,000, you'll be required to complete an owner/builder's course first.

Be aware, too, that it's not always cheaper doing it yourself. The builder will have established relationships with other tradesmen like painters, electricians, plumbers and plasterers who will be part of his team. They will generally charge a conservative rate because of the relationship they have with the builder. However, if you were to contract a plasterer directly, for instance, you probably wouldn't know if you were paying above the going rate or being overcharged.

- **Insurance Agent/Broker.** Insurance is a specialist field with a multitude of players in the market. There are literally hundreds of different insurance packages out there, and finding the right one at the right price to suit your requirements takes more effort than it's worth. Let an agent do this for you. And the best part is that it doesn't cost you anything, as their fee comes as a commission from the insurance underwriters.

- **Property Manager.** As you accumulate investment properties, you'll need a good property manager. They specialise in sourcing good tenants, conducting regular property inspections, and making sure the rent is paid on time. They are well worth the small fee they charge.

Remember, cheap does not mean good! A cheap Property Manager that is badly organised and causes you four weeks vacancy a year through the poor management of tenants and the slack administration of your property, will COST YOU MONEY!

- **Banker**. Brad prefers to deal with the financial institutions himself. There aren't that many around and, once you're into the game, you'll become well aware of current interest rates, packages and trends. Phil and David deal both with institutions directly and through their own Mortgage Banker Leverage Investor Finance (www.leveragefinance.co.nz & www.leveragefinance.com.au) which they set up solely to provide intelligent finance solutions for Real Estate Investors.

There are, of course, others you should include in your team. People like your partners, your family, friends and accountant. The Preferred Suppliers page at www.richmastery.com lists some of the suppliers we recommend.

The next thing you should do is to look at your list, jotting down each team member's strengths and weaknesses. Now look through the list and make a note of any similarities. There could be skills or attributes that are duplicated. Is it possible for you to do without some of these? Now look for skills deficiencies on the list. What skills do you need, but that are missing on your list? Where will you find people that have these skills and how will you make contact with them? Do you even know who the people are that might have this expertise?

> Building your team of experts is an essential part of your Real Estate success. Don't be afraid to dump anyone who isn't performing or pulling in the same direction you are.

▌Your Level Of Risk

> Our lives improve only when we take chances -
> and the first and most difficult risk we can take is to
> be honest with ourselves.
>
> *Walter Anderson*

Another aspect you need to think about before you begin playing the game is to decide on the level of risk you're comfortable with at your particular stage in life. Some people will be prepared to chase higher returns by investing in riskier ventures, while others will take a more conservative approach.

It all depends on your own particular outlook and situation. And it really doesn't matter whether we're talking about Real Estate or the stock market, the principles are the same.

- As an example, here's how we manage our investment portfolios.
- Secure investments: We place 50% to 70% of our investments in safe, secure investments where we are not likely to lose. These should return at least 30% Return On Investment (not yield).
- Speculative investments: We place between 20% and 40% of our investments in higher-return investments. Here, we'd expect to receive a Return On Investment of at least 50%.
- Hare-brained schemes: We never have more than 10% of our investments in these areas. These schemes, if they get off the ground, promise in excess of 100% Returns On Investment.

How do we decide what investment falls into which classification? Well, that's up to you. You decide the rules here. For me, this is how I categorise them:

- Secure investments must guarantee I'll get my money back.
- Speculative investments involve a set of assumptions. I class property that needs to be renovated in this category, because I'm assuming if I fit a new kitchen and bathroom I'll be able to rent it for a certain figure.

Once the renovation is completed the deal could then change to a secure investment.

- Hare-brained schemes are those that I have no control over. I class business here, but others could see this differently.

Once you've decided on what percentage of your investment portfolio you want in which investment risk category, stick to those percentages. Regularly re-evaluate and juggle the amounts to maintain the percentage balance. This is one of the biggest mistakes I see people make. If a hare-brained scheme produces a 100% return one year, they fail to re-invest some of those gains across their other risk categories. The result is usually a massive, and costly, wipe-out if the hare-brained scheme fails later down the line. Continually maintain your percentage spread. Do it at least once a year. We do it after every deal.

As an example, if your rules say you can only have 10% of your $100,000 investment pool in hare-brained schemes, this means you can invest $10,000 in hare-brained schemes. Now if that scheme were to produce a 100% return, giving you a $10,000 profit, you'd end up with $20,000 in the hare-brained scheme. Your rules don't allow this. You'll need to re-assign some of the profit to other categories. Let's ignore the returns from the other categories for the sake of this example. You'll now have a total of $110,000 in your investment portfolio. 10% of this would be $11,000. So you could leave $11,000 in the hare-brained scheme and re-invest the other $9,000 across the other categories in accordance with your rules.

Some people are quite happy buying units/apartments off the plan. They seem to make quite acceptable returns. But to me, (unless I can buy them at an immediate discount) they're hare-brained schemes that I'd rather not get involved in. I'm not saying there's anything wrong with buying directly off the plan; it just depends on what you're comfortable with. If you are buying with the intention to sell at a profit (as many people do, rather than buying and holding as we recommend), be aware that the developer has probably retained a number of the units themselves and is likely to be selling them at the same time as you with a lower acquisition cost and a superior marketing machine.

 WARNING: Russian Roulette With Half The Chambers Loaded

Another hare-brained scheme being promoted by some, is for investors to purchase 5, 10 or 20 units or apartments using Deposit Bonds as the deposit security. The investor does not have the financial ability to settle on the units but *prays and hopes* that during the time the units are being constructed their values will be positively affected by capital growth in the market and increase in value. Investing based on praying and hoping never rates highly with us.

There are several major flaws in this strategy that rarely get told to Russian Roulette players. They are:

What happens when the capital growth in the property market stalls or recedes slightly for a couple of years? Investors are then legally tied into completing the purchase of a number of units that they cannot afford to settle on. Result: Bang – Bankruptcy

Investors are also told by property promoters to… "ride the capital growth wave during construction and sell prior to settlement." There is one big problem with this advice. Often they have given it to most of the investors who have secured property off the plans in the development! What happens when many of the investors in a development put their units back on the market 8 to 12 weeks prior to settlement because none of them have the money to settle? They create a pricing war, where investors are furiously competing against themselves to dump their units fast so they can avoid bankruptcy. The end result is prices fall through the floor and people lose a packet or go bankrupt.

Your level of risk

Real Estate should never be a gamble. Never commit yourself to a deal you haven't got the financial strength to complete.

OK, now that you've given your level of risk some thought, it's time to apply this to the Real Estate market. It's time now to consider how this applies to investing in property, and how it'll affect the way you play the game.

I'm going to explain how you can invest in Real Estate very successfully by means of a model we call the Property Wealth Wheel.

▌The Property Wealth Wheel

> Lampis, the sea commander, being asked how he got his wealth, answered, "My greatest estate I gained easily enough, but the smaller slowly and with much labour."
>
> *Plutarch (A.D. 46?–A.D. c. 120)*

Ever wanted to own a money tree? Who hasn't? Now I know that's just not possible, but there is something very similar. It's a wheel that spins money out forever.

That's right. It's a wheel that, once spinning, will produce a constant income stream no matter what.

What I'm going to show you now is how to put all the theory you've read in this book so far into practice. I'm going to reveal to you the SECRET to creating AMAZING wealth through investing in residential Real Estate.

The Property Wealth Wheel could be the most POWERFUL concept you will ever read. And it's amazingly SIMPLE.

It involves three different types of property deals. They are NEGATIVELY GEARED (Capital Growth) deals, POSITIVE CASHFLOW deals and QUICK CASH deals. But first, you need to understand the different types of deal and how they differ from each other because they have different uses and produce different results.

Negatively Geared (Capital Growth)

Negatively geared deals are those that make a paper or cash LOSS. They are usually found in high value, high capital gain, low rental yield return areas. By this we mean they are top class properties in top class suburbs, but the rental returns are never going to be in the 1.6:1 bracket. What's the significance of this? Well, if the rental return is 1.6 times the purchase price per $1000, the property will probably pay for itself. If it's better than 1.6:1 it will pay for itself and should generate a cash surplus. Negatively geared properties are more likely to be in the 0.8:1 bracket. As an example, on a property that cost you $400,000 you would expect to achieve a rental return of $300 a week. Low rental returns usually need to be compensated for with high capital growth properties.

A low rent area is one where the ratio of rental return is lower than you'd get from a lower class suburb. Just because the property goes up in price doesn't mean the rent goes up correspondingly. Example: if a $100,000 property rents for $150 a week, and a $200,000 property in the same area might rent for $250 a week. Two $100,000 properties will bring you $300 a week combined, yet a $500,000 property will probably earn you only $350 a week.

With a negatively geared (capital growth) property, you can break even with cash, but still make a paper loss. You also need other highly taxable sources of income for negatively geared property deals to be of any benefit.

Positive Cashflow

With positive cashflow deals, the rental income you receive is more than all the cash expenses you incur added together. You still get the paper tax deductions, so you would usually break even on paper. These deals usually involve lower value, lower quality, high rental properties. They are the ones that often don't give you high capital gains, but they will always produce massive returns. They are the properties you buy for their regular income, not their rocketing capital growth prospects. Now you will still get capital growth with these properties, but commonly they are at lower growth levels than the negatively geared (capital growth) property. Capital growth on a positive cashflow property is a handy bonus, but is not the prime reason you buy this type of property.

Sometimes these deals are referred to as being Positively Geared. This is not what I am referring to here. This type of deal is all about CASHFLOW, not gearing. I am talking about properties that produce a positive, and taxable, cashflow.

Quick Cash

Properties we refer to in this category are those we use purely as trading stock. Their primary purpose is for trading, not investing. They're like clothes on the shelf in a clothing shop, only if we get stuck with one or two, we don't worry too much as, unlike clothing, they will increase in value.

These are the properties we buy, spend some money on fixing them up — they could need a coat of paint, a new kitchen, or some new carpets — then sell again. We reinvest the money we make into positive cashflow deals.

It's the quick cash deals that get you going in the first place. These deals can also be used to help generate more, or larger, down payments for other deals.

Bear in mind that Quick Cash deals don't have to be restricted to property. Some people I know buy and sell cars to generate cash to finance their next property deal or renovation. What can you do to raise quick cash that others can't?

The Workings Of The Wheel

The Property Wealth Wheel is a simple concept — it consists of just three components; negatively geared (capital growth) deals, positive cashflow deals and quick cash deals.

The wheel, like any other device, needs to be managed to work efficiently. You will need to manage your portfolio to gain the most from it. You see, you need to constantly ensure your portfolio maintains the right balance. Now I'm not talking about geographic spread or even the balance between units and houses, but rather a balance between the different types of property deals that will produce your income stream.

Aim to do one Quick Cash deal to get you up and running. Then, using the proceeds, buy a Positive Cashflow property, followed by another Quick Cash deal, to help finance your next Positive Cashflow deal. Keep doing this until you have sufficient Positive Cashlow deals in place to make the payments on a Negatively Geared (capital growth) property and purchase one.

An alternative strategy to accumulate your Positive Cashflow property is to buy each one at a substantial discount, creating immediate equity that becomes your deposit to roll into the next property and continue this process over and over again. *Phil and David's web site www.richmastery.com offers a FREE email service that provides discounted property deals to investors and is an excellent tool for purchasing hot deals at a discount. We highly recommend you visit this site, so you can see real life examples of superb Real Estate that is being negotiated every week by Phil and David's property team at massive discounts.*

> People often think you can't purchase property at a discount and frankly that's rubbish. What they mean is THEY can't purchase property at a discount. With the right skills and training anyone can do it. Phil and David run a 3-day **Richmastery Property Academy** where they teach participants exactly how to do this step-by-step. For details on the Academy see their web site.

After following the process outlined above, you should now have four or five Positive Cashflow properties and one that is Negatively Geared. Consider them as an entity.

Here is a pictorial representation of what the Property Wealth Wheel looks like:

Many countries have Capital Gains Tax or a tax on trading property that does not apply to long-term property investments. Because of this you may want to do your Quick Cash deals in another entity (as recommended by your accountant) that is not part of your Property Wealth Wheel because there are no tax advantages in doing so.

Careful planning with a good property accountant can save you thousands of dollars. It's very costly having to reconfigure your property portfolio because you didn't do your homework and purchased Real Estate in the wrong entities. If I had one piece of critical advice for new property investors, it would be to start as you mean to continue and take time out to set up the correct structure from day one.

It is easily possible to establish two Property Wealth Wheels in your first year. Each wheel will then spin off another wheel each year, purely on the equity it will contain.

It's important to remember not to rush out and start buying. You will be excited and eager to get some runs on the board, but you must work according to your plan. This is where your rules come in. Keep reminding yourself of them and what your ultimate outcome is.

Let's assume you have now done all this and you are quite comfortable about how you are going to go about setting up your first Property Wealth Wheel. The first thing you will be looking for is a Quick Cash deal (or a discounted deal if you want to follow the second part of the strategy). You'll begin by doing all the things property buyers do. You'll study the property pages in your local newspaper, look in the windows of Real Estate agent's offices, visit their websites, speak to agents and visit houses that are open for inspection. The more effort here, the better the result.

Now remember, it's a Quick Cash deal you are after. What happens if you come across a great deal – a real beauty that represents great value? Only trouble is, it's a Positive Cashflow house but it's outside your investing rules. What should you do? Pass up a once-in-a-lifetime deal, or buy while the going's good?

You walk away and keep looking.

Don't let your ego, emotions or your enthusiasm distract you from your game plan. You must stick to the rules and look for a Quick Cash deal. If you don't, you're well on your way to becoming an ordinary property owner all over again. Remember the '95 percenters' I spoke about earlier on? Now I know this isn't easy, but if it were, everyone would be doing it, and succeeding.

Another thing to bear in mind is that, with Quick Cash deals, it's all about stock turnover. You see, you have to remember you need to treat this game as you would a business. And business is all about stock turnover. You can buy, renovate and sell a property in six months (assuming you take a month to find a property, a month for the deal to settle, another month to renovate, then a month to re-sell it and a month for that sale to settle.) If you could speed up this process to allow you to do three such deals a year instead of two, it'll make the world of difference. Time is money.

But don't cut corners. I never put a property back on the market until the renovation is complete. This is because potential buyers may still remember it as it was before you bought it and dismiss it without a second look. Remember, they chose not to buy it then, so they'll have preconceived ideas about what could, and what couldn't be done with it.

You see, where I make my money is by changing the property from what it was then to what it is now. That's how I can justify a higher price. It's not often you can buy something, slap on a coat of paint and cut the lawn, then re-sell it for a vastly-increased price. I will generally change the use of the property, change its appearance or change its functionality. And I've often re-sold that very same property back to either the previous vendor or a buyer who had seen it pre-renovation, and got my price, because they didn't see what I saw in it to start with.

This is where the value of being a VICTOR and using my LEFT BRAIN and RIGHT BRAIN (see previous chapters) really pays off. Being open to opportunities allows you to see opportunities others don't.

Understand this: the difference between success and not making it is usually just a fraction. The difference between ORDINARY and EXTRAORDINARY is just the EXTRA.

> The three qualities you need to succeed in life are 10% competence, 10% confidence and 80% clarity. If you understand exactly what you need to achieve, you have a much better chance of achieving it, than if you don't. If you must make a lot of money, how much is that? To some, it's $50,000 a year, but to us, it's more like 10, 20 or $50,000 a day.

Property Wealth Wheel Models

There are a number of different models, or alternatives, of the Property Wealth Wheel that you could customise to suit your individual situation. It all depends on how seriously you want to play the game, what your ultimate goals are and how big you want to grow. A lot also depends on whether you are in business or whether you work for someone else.

You could aim to have two wheels in place that each have, at their cores, Quick Cash deals. You could also develop a Two Wheel Model in which one of them is based on Quick Cash deals and the other on your business. This way, you have a magnificent channel through which to invest the income stream derived from the profits of your business. Now if you have more than one business, develop more Property Wealth Wheel Groups to accommodate your situation. That way you don't have to worry about overseeing many diverse operations. Your business and investment objectives become neatly integrated, saving you time, money and hassle. The objective is to make life easier, not more complicated, isn't it?

This is how your wheels could look:

Property & Business Wealth Wheel

Rich Range Rover ... 4 wheel drive go anywhere

Prosperity Power Porsche

How Much Do You Need?

OK, so you've taken the plunge and decided to build a Property Wealth Wheel. How much money will you need? Here's how you work this out.

Step 1. Write down how much passive income you want to earn each month for the rest of your life.

Step 2. Multiply this by 12 to arrive at an annual income figure.

Step 3. Divide the annual income figure by the annual percentage return you want from your capital assets. This will tell you the size, in dollar terms, of the capital assets you will need.

Step 4. Add to this the amount you will need to invest each year to ensure your income stream (the amount you arrived at in Step 2) isn't eroded by inflation.

Step 5. Add to this figure any amount annually that you want to pass on to your family.

Step 6. Add to this any amount you want to donate to charity each year.

An Example

Step 1. Let's assume you want to earn $15,000 each month in passive income.

Step 2. That's $15,000 X 12 = $180,000 a year.

Step 3. Let's assume you want a 10% return on your capital assets. Now divide $180,000 by 10%. That equals $1,800,000.

Step 4. If you want to protect it against an inflation figure of 5%, then multiply the amount at Step 2 by 5% and add the result to Step 3. $180,000 X 5% = $9,000. $1,800,000 + $9,000 = $1,809,000.

Step 5. If you want to give your family $11,000, then add this amount to the amount arrived at in Step 4. $1,809,000 + $11,000 = $1,820,000.

Step 6. Assume you'd like to donate $10,000 to charity. Add this amount to the amount arrived at in Step 5. $1,820,000 + $10,000 = $1,830,000.

This means you will need an asset base of $1,830,000 to bring in a passive income stream of $15,000 a month.

So now the big question is this: what PERCENTAGE RETURN, or RETURN ON INVESTMENT, will you need from properties you buy to achieve this goal? Here's how you work it out.

Step 1. Write down how much capital you have right now. This is the amount of your net assets.

Step 2. Multiply that amount by 2, and keep doing so, until you arrive at a figure that is as close as possible to the amount you are aiming for.

Step 3. Write down how many times you doubled your initial amount.

Step 4. Write down how many years you have left until you plan on retiring (or until you plan on reaching your goal).

Step 5. Divide the number of years (Step 4) by the number of doubles (Step 3).

Step 6. Divide 72 by the answer you got in Step 5. This will be the percentage return you will need to achieve annually.

This is important, as it will guide you as to how much you need to make out of each deal.

If the result is less than 30%, then I'd suggest you shorten your term or increase the money, because this sort of return you would get from a good Managed Fund. Why bother going to all this trouble for less than 30% return? Let someone else do it for you. To achieve somewhere between 30% and 60% is very realistic, but anything above that takes dedication, effort and commitment.

The figure you've arrived at in Step 6 is most useful – it is the figure that will guide you and help you arrive at a decision when you start actively looking at property. It will tell you if the deal you are looking at meets your long-term goals and requirements.

In addition to this figure, you do need to take into account other factors, such as a figure to maintain a balance in your portfolio (if you have one). If, for instance, your immediate requirement is to buy a speculative investment property, you could afford to risk a deal in which the estimated rate of return is very high. But if you're after something a little more secure to balance your portfolio, you might be satisfied with something that returns a little less than your target figure.

The property wealth wheel

I can't stress the importance of this enough, because it makes the difference between successful investors like myself, and people who end up owning one or two homes. We need to be crystal clear about what we need to achieve before we do any deals – we need to be clear on the outcome.

$$\boxed{\textbf{PART 2}}$$

■ Sourcing Properties

Now it's time to consider how to apply some of this theory to the Game of investing in Real Estate.

Sourcing properties will be the first activity you need to get involved in. You will need to develop a short list of suitable properties to consider. You will use your rules and criteria to decide which of these make it onto your short list and which don't.

So, how do you do this? Where do you start?

The first thing to do is to visit Real Estate agents in the area or areas you want to target. Get to know them. Ask them what stock they have on their books. Keep in touch with them. Phone them every week, as most won't keep in touch with you. Get to know everything about your area – we call it farming your area.

If you don't have the time to do this yourself, you could make use of a Buyer's Agent. They work on behalf of buyers and, for a fee of around 2 to 2?%, they'll do all the legwork and negotiations for you.

Local newspapers are another excellent source. Not only will they tell you what is on the market at the time, they'll also inform you of trends, buying and selling patterns and future market expectations.

Rental Managers are another excellent source who are generally overlooked. You see, there are Real Estate businesses that handle only rental investment properties. They don't sell property at all. If you keep close to them, the time will come (and it frequently does) when an owner wants to sell for whatever reason. They tell the Rental Manager of their intentions. Now if that manager knew you were in the market, they would advise the owner that they could already have a buyer. This would save them the trouble, and expense, of putting it on the market with a traditional Real Estate agent. And because you will probably want to keep the property as a rental, you'd be requiring a Rental Manager, so offer to leave the property with them. They do, after all, know the place and it's history.

Body Corporate Managers are another great source as they are generally one of the first to know when a unit is about to come on the market. And if they knew they would get a quick turnaround of owners of a unit, it would be in their interests to work with you.

Many newspaper and Real Estate company websites have an email notification service where you can enter your desired property details and whenever a property comes on the market that matches your preloaded criteria, an email is generated and sent to you. This is home shopping for Real Estate.

You'll need to develop a good database as you go and keep good records. You don't want to keep phoning up the same person, especially if it's an owner of a property that might be on the rental market. You need to know who you've been in touch with, about which properties, and what the outcome was. You'll be surprised at how confusing this can become once you start working a few areas.

When you're getting started, my advice is not to get too carried away. Keep your income but invest your time doing market research. Drive home using different routes each day to get a feel for what's going on in the area. Phone agents, and get knowledgeable. Farm your area, as they say in the business. That way, agents will treat you seriously.

Keep records on the rental market in your chosen area. When you get a sniff that a property you find suitable may be coming on the market, phone the owner to see if they would be interested in selling. If they are, even remotely, get face-to-face as soon as possible, because if you don't you could lose out because the owner would probably contact the local Real Estate agent for an opinion on what it might be worth. If this should happen, the agent will be pushing for a Sole Agency Agreement, and if they're successful, it will mean a more difficult negotiation and a higher sale price for you. You do need to act very quickly if you ever get a hint that an owner might be interested in selling.

Develop a script, and use it. Jot down all the possible objections an owner may throw at you, and think of responses you'd use to counter them. Refine your script as you go, making additions and corrections from the experience you gain talking to owners and agents. Practice on your family and friends before you get out in the market place. The more you do it, the better it will get. You'll find it an invaluable tool.

Selecting The Right Property

When it comes to selecting the right property to buy, there are a number of things you need to bear in mind. How thorough you are here is going to make all the difference, because you need to remember it's when you buy that you make your profit, not when you eventually sell. Do the right things now and you could be setting yourself up very nicely.

It's more than just being at the right place at the right time. Sure it helps, but here's how you get to know where you need to be, and when:

- **Track market trends**. The first thing you need to understand when investing in Real Estate is what the market is doing. And remember, there's more than one Real Estate market. Different suburbs in different cities could be behaving vastly differently, and you need to understand this. Apart from the general economic trends, there are other equally important factors to bear in mind. For instance, if your chosen area has a leaning towards tenants living, but not sleeping together, you'd be looking for properties that have at least two double-sized bedrooms.

Property investor magazines track these trends and provide detailed analysis of them with valuable investor summaries. Two of the best sources I have found are www.apimagazine.com.au (Australian Property Investor Magazine) and www.kpimagazine.co.nz (Kiwi Property Investor Magazine). Subscribe to these magazines; they are essential resources for every property investor. Contact your newsagent to find out about the local property investor magazine in your country.

Scan the internet, and keep your eye on the local papers, after a while you'll start accumulating all sorts of useful information that will help crystallise your decision-making.

- **Study the available land supply in your chosen area**. Real Estate is all about supply and demand. Identify where the developers are working and ascertain the ramifications of their developments on supply and demand in your area. Be on the lookout for prime property, which will appreciate in time. Features that will ensure this are: water frontage, river frontage, hills, views and proximity to amenities and transport. This type of property is excellent for your 'long-term holds' and will traditionally provide great capital growth. If it's cashflow you're after, concentrate on the mid to low end of the market. Average properties in average neighbourhoods usually work well. But don't exclude yourself from a diamond deal that is out there sitting in a capital growth hotspot and churning out cashflow. Those deals are much harder to find, but be open to them because you need to act fast when they come your way.

But how do you do this if the area you're targeting is new to you? You know, somewhere on the other side of the country, for instance. I always phone the president of the Real Estate Institute for that area and offer to pay for an hour or so of their time. This way I get the inside track, and because this person is always a Real Estate agent, I've never been charged. I explain I'm over to buy some investment properties and need to know the current hot spots, market movement, trends, top capital growth and cashflow areas, and any other recommendations he or she might have. People like this are an encyclopaedia of local property knowledge; make sure you leverage their expertise and use every minute of your time with the wisely.

- **Order of sale**. You need to understand how your chosen marketplace reacts when it starts moving. What type of properties sell first? What will follow? Normally average houses go first because people moving into an area just want to get in to get to know it better before buying a decent place. Once average homes start selling well, town-houses usually follow. Next will be development sites and 'renovator's delights'. These are my rules, but yours may be different, depending on the area you're operating in. Be guided by what you believe will happen in your area. If you want to buy a home to renovate, you need to jump into the market pretty early, otherwise you'll be looking for the proverbial needle in a haystack. This is why you need to understand the order of sale. You've probably heard about buying the worst house in the best street. It's a great idea, and you can generally make a few dollars if you don't pay too much and avoid risks like overcapitalising or taking too long on the renovations.

- **Understand your game plan.** The key to selecting the right property is to understand what you're looking for at the time. You must be very clear about what you're after. This takes discipline, but it's the one sure way you'll achieve your long-term Real Estate goals.

Are you after a Quick Cash deal, a Negative Geared (capital growth) property, a Positive Cashflow property, a Discounted Cashflow or a Discounted Negatively Geared property?

Suppose you were just starting out and wanted a Quick Cash deal to get you going. Suppose too, you came across this fantastic Positive Cashflow property while you were out looking for your Quick Cash deal. What would you do? Would you make an offer? NO, you'd keep looking because it's not what you're after.

But suppose you were after a Negative Cashflow property and you stumbled across this great Quick Cash deal. What should you do? In this case, you should buy, because Quick Cash deals are like finding money in the road. Buy and turn it around as you would any Quick Cash deal, as it will provide cash for your Negative Cashflow property when it comes along.

Understand what YOUR requirements are. Sit down and work out what you need to do to achieve your goals. Set your path and go for it!

Don't chase the market. Too many people try to 'pray and hope' their way to wealth, and crash and burn when it all goes against them. When the taxi driver knows the property market is booming and is telling you to buy, it's time to take time out and wait for the market crash.

The best time to buy Real Estate is when no one else is!

- **Understanding your buyer.** This is one of the keys to my success. I understand who's going to buy my properties. The first thought when I look at a property is who's going to buy it. If I can ascertain this, then I'm in a good position to renovate the property so that it becomes attractive to these types of buyers or renters. Let's work through an example to illustrate this.

Suppose I see a unit that I believe can be made attractive to a single lady. What are the features she would be looking for? Security, a lock-up garage with electric doors, a trendy appearance, and a private balcony or courtyard. I then assess the unit with regard to what renovations need to be completed to deliver these key outcomes.

I then get a rental assessment on the unit from a local Property Manager to confirm what the rent would be if the unit were in its renovated state. Next I get a Valuer to give me a sale price assessment of the unit based on my anticipated improvements.

Now I do two things:

I work the whole process backwards…

Renovated Unit Sale Price Assessment was:	**$185,000**
Less My Profit	$ 20,000
Less Renovation Costs	$ 22,000
Less Purchasing & Resale Expenses	$ 17,000
Balance Left	**$126,000**

Now I know $126,000 is my ceiling purchase price for this Quick Cash Deal. Every dollar I negotiate to purchase the property below that price is money in my back pocket. If the seller wants more than $126,000 I walk away from the deal!

The second thing I do is assess my fallback position…

I drop all the numbers for the property into the Richmastery Property Analysis software (available from www.richmastery.com) and get a financial property summary. See page 111 for an example of what this looks like.

I do this to find out what the financial performance of the property would be if I kept it in my property portfolio, or if I had to rent it out for reasons beyond my control if I couldn't sell it. My intention may not be to keep the property, but if things go wrong, I want the comfort of knowing I have a backup plan that won't send me broke.

Don't fall into the trap of looking at a property and saying, "Gee, I would make this place look like a million dollars by doing this, this and this." One of the most dangerous things in doing Quick Cash Deals is that your ego gets involved and you end up over-capitalising a property and then can't sell it for enough to cover the costs you have incurred. It's only the figures that count; nothing else matters, including your ego!

> *The golden rule of Quick Cash Deals is:* Understand who's going to buy the property from you first.

So, is there an art to selecting the right property? No, not really. We recommend you develop a check sheet that reminds you what your rules are and what specifically you are looking for.

▌Doing The Numbers

> Do not worry about your difficulties in Mathematics. I can assure you mine are still greater.
>
> *Albert Einstein (1879 - 1955)*

Before you commit yourself to any property, you need to satisfy yourself that the deal meets your investment criteria and will deliver the end result you desire.

You need to do the numbers; do them accurately and do them well.

This is particularly important when you are spending money on the property with renovations. In the last chapter we talked about controlling your ego. The best way to do this is to control the spending on the project. It's so easy to over-capitalise a property. In fact, it's one of the biggest traps new investors fall into.

Often I get asked by young couples whether they should buy an investment property OR buy their own home and then an investment property. My answer may surprise you. I always recommend they buy the investment property first! Why? Because every time a couple purchases their own home, what do they want to do with it? Improve, renovate, change, paint, etc. Without even knowing it, they spend all their surplus cash on their home because they are emotionally attached to it.

The benefits of getting into an investment property first are:

a) You can leverage the equity in your first investment property to buy other properties. The first deal is always the hardest; getting a roll on with other investment properties from there is a piece of cake.

b) Your strongest motivation will always be to establish your own home. By making the hard decision first to get an investment property, you maintain and heighten your passion and drive to save for your first home.

There are too many casualties who have got carried away with renovations and before they know it, their profit's gone into thin air. Costing renovations can be particularly difficult because, if you're looking at nine or ten properties all of which have potential, what builder is going to have the time to give you fairly accurate quotes on them all? They just don't have the time for speculative business (from their point of view, that is). So where does that leave you?

This is what we do. I've developed a close working relationship with a few good builders, and they have given me a very good rough idea of what it costs to carry out certain jobs like tiling, erecting a new fence, painting or putting in a new bathroom. These figures I use myself to get a rough idea of what any combination of renovation work might cost.

> I then feed these numbers, along with all the others I have, into a computer program designed to produce reports and financial statements to help me decide if the property will produce the results I expect.

The software program I use is called **Richmastery Property Analysis**, and it's available from www.richmastery.com. I feed in figures such as the purchase price, the cost of legals, searches and inspections, renovations, the rent it returns, agent's fees and commissions, depreciation, Body Corporate fees, maintenance costs, interest and inflation rates. It produces a whole raft of reports such as full financial statements, reports on deductions and expenses, tax credits, 10-year equity projections and much more. These are invaluable when talking to the bank about finance arrangements. They help me get the best deal I can, because it pre-frames the bank according to the criteria I have used to making the deal profitable. I use the software package to massage the numbers by running through various financial scenarios beforehand. That way I can quickly ascertain whether the deal will suit my purposes. If I can't get it to work by meeting my criteria, I dump it and move on.

I have found this program to be invaluable because it enables me to know my limits and the project outcome before I start. This way I don't waste time on dud deals, because they are screened out before I even start. There are several other programs around but the Richmastery Property Analysis Software is the only one that provides some key financial indices that are critical to my financial decision-making.

I load in the key data information below along with some details that allow me to estimate depreciation and input mortgage interest rates.

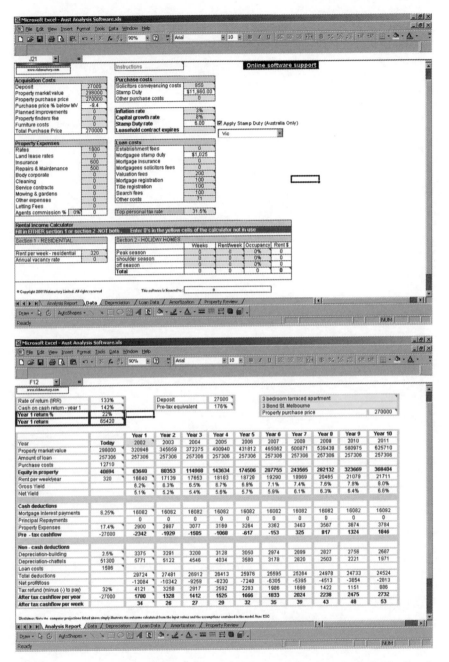

The Property Analysis Report that I can then produce on each deal takes 2 minutes to calculate and provides me with all the information I need to make the purchase decision. If the numbers don't stack up, I know I need to negotiate a better deal or walk away.

▌ Negotiating The Deal

> The difference between a moral man and a man of honour is that the latter regrets a discreditable act, even when it has worked and he has not been caught.
>
> *H. L. Mencken (1880 - 1956),*
> *'Prejudices: Fourth Series,' 1924*

Negotiating the deal is the most important activity in Real Estate because it's where you make your money. **Understand this**: Buying right can make you; buying wrong can break you. If there is one thing you need to understand in Real Estate, it's how to negotiate well.

> Good negotiation will result in you achieving what YOU want, regardless of the seller's circumstances. Your job is to get your price or walk away! There are always more deals out there waiting for you. Too many buyers pay too much for properties, because they were not prepared to walk away from a deal.

Auctions are a classic for this, and that's why agents love them!

It's important to control your emotions and drive the negotiation process – you have the upper hand.

Remember you're calling the shots; sit back and watch the seller react. You are very definitely in a position of strength, so use it wisely. Build into your offer everything you need to make it attractive to you.

I like to think of the negotiating process as the art of making the seller happily give you what you want.

So how do you do that?

- Start off by fully understanding their motivation for selling. Listen very carefully to what the seller says. Ask why they are selling. Is it to move out of town, because they are getting divorced, or upgrading to a larger house? Put yourself in their position and understand the pressures they would be under.

Remember, an estate agent will very often put words in the seller's mouth or represent the situation differently to package it in a much more politically correct way. But there is one thing agents are good at: TALKING. If you let them, they will go on for hours. Use the agent's weakness (their big mouth) and let them talk the legs off a donkey while you sweetly extract all the intelligence you need about the seller.

Having said that, I don't believe negotiating is a war. No one dies! Although I have caused a few heart attacks with some of my offers. No one has ever lost a limb.

I believe negotiating is nothing more than working through discussions (written or verbal) with the seller until you understand what their REAL motivation for selling is. Then you're home and dry. Understand this: As long as you satisfy their REAL reason for selling, they'll give on everything else and often the price is the first casualty. It's human nature.

My favourite deals are those with motivated vendors – sellers who have a very motivating reason to sell. There are six types of motivated vendors.

The 6 D's of Motivated Vendors:

Death (Deceased Estates)

Divorce

D' Bank

Dummies (People who don't know how much their property is worth)

Deadlines (Anyone who has to sell by a certain date, eg moving overseas)

Developers

 These people are ready and waiting to give you a property at a very cheap price, if you can find them and negotiate well.

Opportunity Knocks 1: I was farming an area one week and came across a great opportunity. The opportunity wasn't as much the house, as it was the person selling it. It was a nice three-bedroom home in a good area with average capital growth and a healthy Positive (pre-tax) cashflow.

But Yappie, the agent who could not shut up, told me the house had been on the market for four months, the owner had accepted two previous offers for $110,000 (it was worth $125,000) but both previous offers had fallen over because the buyers couldn't get finance. What a shame, I thought! But it got better. The owner's wife had moved to the new house up north four months earlier and her husband was staying with the old house until it was sold. They were 400 kilometres apart and had been for four months. What a shame, I thought!

I told Yappie the Real Estate agent that I wanted to put in an offer for $95,000 ($30,000 / 20%+ below market value). She said she would phone the seller and see if he would accept that. Yappie talked and the owner balked and I was told there is no way he will accept $95,000. I told Yappie I wanted to put a formal written offer in for $95,000. Despite her moans and groans she prepared the Sale Agreement and I signed it.

Later that afternoon, Yappie phoned me to tell me my offer had been accepted!

What happened during that day that changed the seller's mind?

- He realised he may have to wait a long time for another offer if he didn't accept mine.

- He realised that even if he got other offers, they too might fall over as the first two had.

- He thought about how lonely he was and how much he missed his wife.

- He thought about the possibility of being without her for another four months.

- He realised solving his problem was more important that a few extra dollars.

There are two big lessons here:

Lesson 1 - Written Contracts Change Minds: A seller's emotions really hit hardest when a written contract is in their hand. Somehow offers aren't real unless they are in writing sitting in front of you. It's easy to be macho when it's all talk, but much harder when it's on your table in black and white. When that happens a seller's brain has strange things happen to it – it goes all mushy. They have to make a decision then and there. It's just them, Yappie (who is only interested in their commission cheque) and the deal.

Lesson 2 - Time Erodes Certainty: This is a biggie. The more time you give a seller, the more negotiable they become and the more power you have. Time is your greatest weapon, so use it wisely.

Opportunity Knocks 2: I was looking to do this great deal and had a meeting with the seller I was negotiating with. I thought it went well. When it came to the second meeting I was pretty sure we had it in the bag but, blow me down, he told me he had thought about things and had decided not to sell.

I didn't cry on the table but my heart sank. Ever gone from a euphoric high to a basement low? It's gut wrenching!

Not one to be beaten, I went back to my office and formulated a battle plan.

Phase 1: I sent him an email, thanking him for the meeting and issuing him with 14 days notice to change his mind before I launched a deal that would compete against him and inevitably lose him some money. Was I serious? Yes! Did I want to carry out my persuasive threat? No.

Phase 2: I wrote up and pre-signed a Sale Agreement, then stapled a cheque for a $100,000 deposit to it. Then I went down to a local gift basket shop and ordered a $500 gift basket. When was the last time you have seen a $500 gift basket? Believe me, they look impressive! I put the cheque and the Sale Agreement in an envelope and put them in the gift basket with a card that said: 'Congratulations on selling your xyz to us. Attached is a gift basket (for you to share this exciting moment with your family), our deposit cheque for $100,000 (which you can cash immediately) and the Sale Agreement that you just need to sign and return to us in the courier envelope provided."

Guess what happened? By 10 o'clock the next morning he had accepted the deal, banked the cheque and was on his way to his solicitor to complete the agreement!

So, what are the lessons? Certainly Lessons 1 and 2 but also:

Lesson 3 - Money In The Hand Is A Power Tool: A $100,000 cheque in your hand creates all sorts of emotions like .... imagine what I could do with this ... new car, better house, overseas trip. The mind goes wild dreaming dreams and exploring all possibilities.

Let me put it this way. If you were selling a property and had two offers, one with a deposit cheque and one without, which one would you take? I have used this tactic over and over again with amazing results.

Now understand you won't get a strike every time, but you will get good results and often you'll surprise yourself. Was it worth me risking a $500 gift basket to turn a losing deal into a winning one? Absolutely!

Lesson 4 – Family Pressure Is Hard To Say No To: What do you think would have happened when the $500 gift basket arrived? Everyone would have come running with comments like ... "Wow that's cool, I want the chocolates." "Who sent it, Dad?" "You must have really been good to someone."

Now what's the wife thinking? "I want to know who this is from 'cause it had better not be from another woman."

Hubby opens the card in front of the wife, because he has nothing to hide. She sees the cheque. Now the game goes to a whole 'nuther level (as I intended). Why? Because she's now thinking of all the pairs of shoes she can buy and planning the dream family holiday they have always wanted. She wants to take the money and run. I have won an ally inside his own home that I hadn't even met! Isn't life beautiful!

Now hubby has a dilemma. If he doesn't do the deal with me, he is going to feel guilty eating the gift basket and should probably send it back. But to do that would create difficulties with his family. He is also going to have to battle with his wife and explain why he has to send back the $100,000 cheque.

The end result? It's easier to say yes than it is to say no. Game, set and match!

- Understand Neuro-Linguistic Programming.

I'm now going to introduce another concept that has to do with negotiating in the broad sense. It's called Neuro-Linguistic Programming, or NLP for short. NLP is a model of human behavior and communication that draws from the knowledge of psychodynamics and behavioral theories. It is concerned with the identification of both conscious and unconscious patterns in communication and behavior and how they interact in the process of change.

So what does this mean as far as negotiating is concerned?

If we can understand the three key components of NLP, we can become better negotiators. These are:

a) Rapport and communication. Rapport and communication covers areas such as language- representational systems, eye-accessing movements, verbal and nonverbal pacing and leading, communication translation skills, and representational system overlapping.

b) Gathering information. Understanding NLP allows us to understand the processes people use to encode and transfer their experience and to guide and modify their behaviour. All the information gathering we do is done through three sensory systems: the visual, the auditory, and kinesthetic (feeling and touching). And to a lesser extent, we also use our senses of smell and taste, but these are not of any significance. But the really interesting thing here is that visual accounts for 40% of the way we communicate, auditory only 20% and kinesthetic 40%. Isn't that interesting?

c) Change strategies and interventions. So, what does this mean for us as negotiators? Well, one of the big lessons here is to learn to match the language system used by the person you're negotiating with. That way you build rapport really quickly. But be careful not to mimic their language – rather match and mirror the way they communicate.

Successful negotiators also understand the various behavioural styles people have. They understand people fall into one of four main behavioural groups. They can be either outgoing in nature, or reserved. Or they can be either task-oriented or people-oriented.

- Be empathetic. Look around for clues. Pick up on things that are important to the seller. Look for, and understand, what it is they cherish. Let me give you an example.

I walked into this house once and immediately noticed this beautiful family portrait hanging in the entrance hall. I could see it was worth a lot to the owners, so I insisted it form part of the deal. I argued that it looks so good where it is and the entrance hall just wouldn't look the same without it. I knew that if the owner wanted to exclude it, it would be worth, to me, probably between $5,000 and $10,000. You see, from here on in, they'll stop negotiating about the price and start negotiating about what's important to them.

When I walk into a place, the first thing I always say is, "This is incredible! I wasn't expecting anything like this. I just love that main road out the front." Where does that leave the seller? He would probably have been dreading overcoming objections to the main road, and would have no room for manoeuvre. You see, his whole negotiating strategy would have been developed to deal with it as an issue, and now it would have been turned upside down. This leaves him with only one thing left to talk about – the price. This brings us back to the basics. Remember what I said about the different perceptions buyers and sellers have about the selling process? Sellers sell on value, but buyers buy on price. You need to get them firmly away from the 'value' plain and place them squarely in the 'price' plain. This is your territory. It's where you call the shots. You are in charge of the encounter. Of course, when you're selling, you'll be aiming to get the buyer all emotionally involved, as this is 'value' territory.

- Another strategy is to play dumb and ask the seller to help you put the deal together. Sellers will not say no because their egos will get in the way. Mention that since they've sold well before, perhaps they can assist you with this deal. You could, for instance, ask the seller to leave $10,000 in the deal because the building inspection has shown more work is required to bring the property up to a finished standard than you originally estimated. This could very often be better than losing the sale. If you're smart, you'll negotiate the $10,000 discount as the deposit so you don't have to come up with one. Or you could structure it in such a way that the seller leaves the $10,000 in the deal for twelve months, and then you pay them back. If you're doing a Quick Cash deal, you would have sold the property by this point and if you were doing a Negatively Geared or a Positive Cashflow property, you would have re-financed the original mortgage and got an extra $10,000 out anyway.

I'm a real fan of creative financing that turns good deals into exceptional ones. You are only limited by the possibilities your mind can come up with.

There are a few rules I have when negotiating deals that I NEVER break. They are:

- I never submit an unconditional cash offer unless the seller is under massive time pressure to sell by a deadline. In this case I do my due diligence, give them a low unconditional cash offer and in the odd case, attach a nice healthy deposit cheque.

  The reason I never submit an unconditional cash offer unless the above circumstances present themselves, is because it leaves me no room to negotiate.

- I never buy at auction because that way I can't do my homework first. I can't conduct the necessary pest and building inspections or any other due diligence checks and too many people get carried away emotionally and pay more than the property is worth.

  On top of this, agents stack the cards against you by using dummy bidders, agent bidders, or vendor bidders. Many Real Estate companies have a policy that they will not engage in these dodgy tactics and in many locations these sorts of shenanigans are banned by law. But the reality is it does happen, it's hard to prove and it is a risk.

  Auctions shift the power from the buyer to the seller, and I don't like being involved in any process I don't control. The **Richmastery Property Academy** teaches seven advanced strategies of how to win at auctions.

> **Understand this**: Agents love auctions because it gives them a load of advertising (you need a good vendor-pays advertising package to run an auction), and it puts the property on the market without a price. They can then use this as an excuse when it doesn't sell. They will try very hard indeed to get the vendor to sell for far less than it's worth on the day of the auction. It's called 'vendor-bashing' in the industry.

Be aware that you are still in the negotiation phase of the process until the deal becomes unconditional and all the clauses that your offer was 'subject to' become fulfilled. Always include conditions in every offer.

Some of the favourite clauses we use are:

- Due Diligence Clauses
- Access Clauses
- Facsimile Clauses
- Vendor Finance Clauses
- Renovation and Improvements Clauses

> The **Richmastery Acquisition Software** contains all the clauses we recommend investors use. You can cut and paste them straight out of the software and use them on your Sale Agreements.

We use clauses to protect and safeguard us in the negotiation and it provides a lever where we can buy extra time if we need to:

Here's what I mean:

Suppose I came across this real beauty that I knew would sell like hot cakes. Let's also suppose it's one of those deals that I need to do straight away or I'll lose it. How do I buy myself enough time to 'do the numbers'?

I explain to the seller that I really love the place, and I'm quite happy to put forward a cash contract for the asking price, but I really can't make such a decision without first showing the property to my wife. Now as she's out of town and won't be back for another week, I'm more than happy to submit a cash offer, subject only to my wife seeing the place and agreeing to the purchase within seven days. Very few sellers will pass up an offer like that.

This takes the property off the market, giving me time to run through my figures and carry out the necessary checks. If the deal doesn't stack up, I can still pull out simply by having my wife reject the deal. Oh, it's a good idea to have a wife otherwise legally you may have a hard time getting out of the contract. Partner or business partner works equally as well.

▌Financing The Deal

> Finance is the art of passing currency from hand to hand until it finally disappears.
>
> *Robert W. Sarnoff*

There are many ways to finance your deals. Some of them are obvious, others aren't. Which type you choose largely depends on you. But if you're not smart about this, you could end up like most investors and only ever own one or two investment properties.

You need to apply a large measure of lateral thinking here, because if you can't finance a deal, it's no deal. You can make all the offers you like, but unless you can come up with the money, you're wasting your time.

So how do you go about this? How do you finance a deal?

The simple answer is any way you can.

Consider all your options. These include:

- *Equity* you may already have in an existing property. Make your home work for you. It's probably the cheapest money you'll ever come across. The question you need to ask is how much interest is the equity in your home earning you right now? Unless you're using it to purchase other property, the answer is none!

- *Refinance* an existing property. This is a great method for raising money. We follow one of these four strategies when we are doing a deal so we can refinance the property within six months and get our money back.

  a) Buy, renovate and refinance

  b) Buy at a discount and refinance

  c) Buy and change the property's use and refinance

  d) Buy in a High Capital Growth area, ride the property value up, and refinance

Financing the deal

- *Vendor Finance.* This is not commonly used but it's a great finance option and we have personally done numerous vendor finance deals. Simply put, the vendor sells the property to you for $300,000 and they agree to vendor finance $50,000 of the purchase price at 7.5% for 12 months. This means you have a Sale Contract for $300,000 on which just about any bank will loan you 80% ($240,000). This means you only need to come up with $10,000 to do the deal: Settlement Day: $250,000 required, Bank Mortgage: $240,000, Amount required by you: $10,000.

  There are many vendors who do not have an immediate need for the all of the proceeds of the sale of a property. They may be retired people, financially independent or have other reasons. Nevertheless, they may be willing to leave in a portion of the purchase price (say 10% or 20%) for a 6 or 12-month period. If you can provide a genuine reason for needing the finance, such as "I have the extra $20,000 but I want to invest it in renovations and cosmetic improvements to the property to maximise its value," then a vendor will often be prepared to assist you. The bank is very happy for you to use other people's money for financing, as they are still first in the list with security over the title.

  The best use of vendor finance is on sellers who are either motivated vendors (the 6 D's) or have made substantial profit on the property and are prepared to vendor finance a purchaser into a property so they can realise their profit. See the Richmastery Acquisition Software for the exact vendor finance clause we use.

- *Subsidised Deposit or Vendor Gifting.* This is similar to vendor financing, but it involves the seller giving you a discount for an early settlement. This is normally a separate agreement to the Sale Agreement and can have some nasty tax implications for the seller if not structured correctly.

- *Personal Loans.* Don't overlook these. They are most useful for paying for things like deposits, refurbishments and renovations. Most banks have the facility to give personal loans to their customers.

- *Credit cards.* Another great way to finance deposits, refurbishments or renovations. Many successful investors use their 55-day interest-free credit cards for their Quick Cash deals, knowing they will have sold the property by the time the money is due.

There are many institutions that will advance you the money to finance your Real Estate deals. Apart from the major banks, there is a whole raft of second tier lenders who aggressively chase new business. I deal with a wide range of them and am very satisfied with the results. Of course, some deals I do involve higher-than-normal interest rates, high establishment fees and early exit penalties.

My point here is that I don't particularly care about these things, as long as I know about them when I do the deal. You see, if I factor them into my calculations so that I still make a profit, that's fine. I don't begrudge any lender their share of the profits, if I achieve my objective with my deal. In many cases, I'm faced with the choice of making an acceptable profit or no profit at all. The fact that the lender makes a healthy profit as well doesn't bother me.

Let me give you another example of creative thinking when structuring a deal.

I recently negotiated a property that involved five 2-bedroomed holiday flats and a vacant block of land. The owner needed to sell. He was asking $440,000 for the lot. The units and holiday flat were returning him an income of around $51,000 a year.

My offer was $350,000 for the units. And because the bank would only lend me 80% of the purchase price ($280,000), I wanted vendor finance of $70,000 to cover the rest. This would mean I didn't have to outlay any money.

At first the vendor was sceptical, saying he was short of cash and would need to get a full time job. But my calculations hinged on the assumption I wasn't going to outlay any capital. So I then played my trump card – in addition to the $350,000 for the units ($280,000 from the bank and $70,000 vendor financed) I offered $160,000 for the vacant land with settlement in a year's time.

This meant he'd achieve $510,000 for both the units and the land instead of his asking price of $440,000. The difference, I explained, being the $70,000 I was asking for as vendor finance. And to clinch the deal, I explained this amount would be deducted from the payment for the land at the time of settlement, bringing the total figure back down to his original asking price. That way I'd get my 'no cash down' deal and he would get his asking price, plus he wouldn't have to find a full time job.

Financing the deal

The end result was a sweet deal that suited everyone. I'm now planning on developing the vacant land.

Don't disregard solicitor's trust funds when weighing up your finance options either. They can be a good source of ready capital, particularly for the short-term. Another source is other investors, but I'll only consider them under my terms. Most will generally want a say in how you run or structure your business affairs. This I'll never agree to. As long as they only want to inject funds and then reap a return at the end, that's fine. Nothing else. Most are just not worth the hassle.

If you borrow from family members, make sure you have an agreement in place. This is important because as time goes by, people's needs change. And their recall of what you originally agreed often becomes coloured or blurred. Things can also go wrong or not turn out as you expected. No deal is airtight so make sure you use your solicitor to document agreements and have robust commercial processes that protect everyone.

There are many other ways to fund your deals. I am going to show you some of the not-so-obvious ones now. These are commonly used and they work very well.

The **first method** is very useful as it turns $40,000 into $140,000 every year, without fail. This is how:

I start off with $40,000 and aim to use it to buy an $80,000 unit. To achieve this, the bank will want me to put down 20% as a deposit. That's $16,000. They will then lend me $64,000.

OK, so out of my initial $40,000, I've spent $16,000 on the deposit. I then allocate $18,000 for renovations and a further $2,000 for transaction and sundry costs. That leaves me with $4,000 liquidity from my initial $40,000.

Now, an $80,000 property that has had $18,000 spent on it wisely will increase in value to around $120,000 in most areas, and that's being conservative. I then organise a revaluation with a valuer who is approved by the bank with which I want to refinance. Once the valuation is complete I re-finance the unit, and borrow the 80% that they will lend me on it. That's $96,000. To this I add my $4,000 left over from my initial $40,000 kitty. That gives me $100,000. I've now got all my money back from the property and I still own the unit.

This gives me two options. Add it to my Real Estate portfolio if the figures stack up or sell it as a Quick Cash deal. Because it usually takes one month to renovate a property, one month to sell it and one month for the sale to settle, I can comfortably repeat this cycle four times each year doing Quick Cash deals.

On this deal I will make $20,000 profit when I resell the unit for $120,000. Add this to my initial $40,000, which I recovered from the sale, and I now have $60,000 to play with when I buy my next unit. Using the same basic criteria as before, I buy, refurbish, refinance then resell the second and make another $20,000 profit. Only this time, once I have recovered my initial $60,000, I now have $80,000 to play with on my third purchase of the year. I now have enough in the kitty to allow me to buy two properties this time and not just one. Same scenario again results in a $40,000 profit when I sell, and I get $120,000 to finance my next round of purchases. I now buy three properties of similar value and land up with $180,000 after they have been finally sold. Along the way I will have outlaid somewhere in the region of $40,000 in commissions, duty and other related expenses, leaving me with a profit of $140,000 for the year.

Method two involves hanging on to the properties I've just bought and not selling them. I keep my stock. Here again, I spend one month renovating the property before going back and getting it revalued. I then refinance and use that money to acquire the next property.

This I can do ten times a year, with the result that my initial $40,000 will end up purchasing me around $1,200,000 in property a year (10 properties x an average property valuation of $120,000). That's not a bad year. But it gets better. Remember each property only cost me $100,000 and I got all my money out. That means I have $200,000 in equity (10 properties x $20,000 equity per property) And I still have the $40,000 I started with.

In effect we have now turned $40,000 into $240,000 in 1 year. A 600% return. Try and find that in the stock market.

Most people simply don't do this because they believe they don't have the borrowing capacity but in reality most do, if they'd only ask and make sure they structure their purchases intelligently.

Method three is much easier than the previous two. It hinges around investing the original $40,000 into a fixed deposit account at the bank. Now the bank will again lend $64,000 on security of the property. I then ask for a line of credit on the $40,000 deposit, which gives me a total amount of $104,000 to play with (my $40,000 deposit plus the $64,000 the bank loans me against the property).

I purchase the property for $80,000, renovate as usual, and then refinance, depositing the profit and the original $40,000 back into my line of credit account.

Then I withdraw my $40,000 from the line of credit account and start the cycle all over again. The beauty of this method is there is no refinancing, stamp duty (non applicable in New Zealand) or other costs. This is because we are just using the line of credit account and aren't selling the property; we just refinance and let it sit in our property portfolio.

This will give you some idea of the different strategies you could use to create your Property Wealth Wheel.

What do I do? I do whatever I can. But whatever route I take for each deal, I still observe my basic rules, which are:

- Quick Cash Deals are normally funded by a Line of Credit or Fixed Term Deposit.

- All Positive Cashflow Properties are bought on Interest Only Loans fixed for a term of at least 5 years - but preferably 20 years.

- Negatively Geared (capital growth) property is bought on a Line of Credit or Part Line of Credit, with a part of the loan on a fixed interest rate and the rest floating to minimise the interest I am charged.

- ALL rent and payments received from the properties go through the Line of Credit - nothing else is paid for by this company or trust.

- Build enough equity and re-draw against the high capital growth Negatively Geared Property to start another Wealth Wheel.

- Invest the re-drawn amount in a term deposit and use this as collateral so there is no transfer of funds.

> I NEVER, EVER cross-collateralize. I NEVER, EVER give my asset company as security for something my trading company wants to fund. It is important that you maintain a clear structural separation between your investment property portfolio and your property trading activities.

The worst thing that can happen is that you mix them all up in one big pot and get taxed to death because you didn't take the time to structure your entities correctly. Preparation pays!

Dealing with Bankers

Dealing with bankers or brokers can be a challenge for many investors, and yet it's one of the critical aspects of investing to master. It does not matter how many deals you can negotiate if you cannot get the funding to purchase them.

As the say, "When in Rome, do as the Romans do." When dealing with bankers, act as the bankers act! I have found that the more you understand how bankers think, and what they are looking for, the easier it is to get their approval for more of their money.

Banks have three questions they need answered when they lend to you:

Is their money safe?

Can they make a profit from lending to you?

Will you be competent at managing their money?

The 4 C's of Borrowing

In the banking and mortgage lending business, there is a rule-of-thumb called The 4 C's. These are qualities banks want to see when they consider loaning you money.

Financing the deal

Here are the 4 C's of Borrowing ...

Credit: A banker wants to determine that you are a good credit risk by seeing your current credit picture: a 'snap-shot' of your past and present debt, current available credit, and a rating of your debt repayment history.

Capacity: This is simply a measure of your financial capacity to pay the loan. This is measured by dividing your gross monthly income by the amount you are paying to service your total outstanding debts (including the new payment of the property you are planning to buy). Generally, bankers will allow up to 35% of your monthly income to be used for your housing or investment property expense and all other current obligations you have outstanding including credit cards, auto loans, student loans, etc.

Collateral: This is the valuation of the property you're about to purchase. The banker needs to know the value of the property you are 'pledging' as collateral for the loan.

Character: Generally, to determine character, banks look at your job stability, your probability of continued employment, and the soundness of your financial habits.

Remember – bankers are trained to look for the reason to say NO, not YES. Banks will judge you on everything from your clothes to your proposal – your proposal tells them how serious you are, and it gives them all the information they need to say yes.

- Give them everything they need to say YES! Your financial presentation is everything.
- Never lie, you will eventually be found out, and may find it difficult to get finance in the future with a black mark on your file.
- Spread your loans around more than one bank.

    That way if you need an extra $10,000 it's easy to get $2000 unsecured from five banks, than $10,000 from one bank.

    It's also good for asset protection and avoids one bank cross guaranteeing all mortgages with all properties, which can start a domino effect if you go through a difficult patch and the bank calls in some of their mortgages.

- Your proposal should impress them and demonstrate your commitment. They love lots of figures, and so do their analysts.

Phil and David use the **Richmastery Property Acquisition Software** (available at www.richmastery.com) for preparing and presenting their finance proposals to banks.

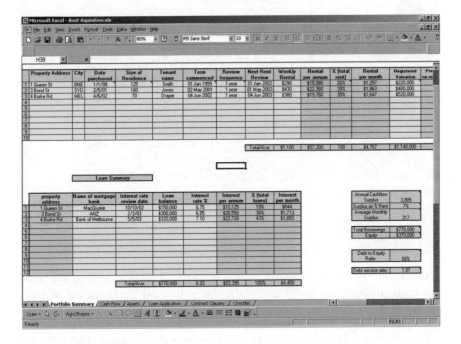

This program is designed to make the acquisition of your property investment simple and time efficient. It helps you with writing contracts, a checklist of all the things to action from signing the contract through to settlement day, a comprehensive program that summarises your property portfolio, cash-flow forecast, assets and liabilities, along with a mortgage application form, and a proposal for finance template that just does not get declined!

The Property Portfolio Summary report quickly shows the banker key financial information for each of the investment properties I own, along with the financial ratios such as the Debt Service Ratio and Debt to Equity Ratio that they need to know to tick the boxes on their approval list.

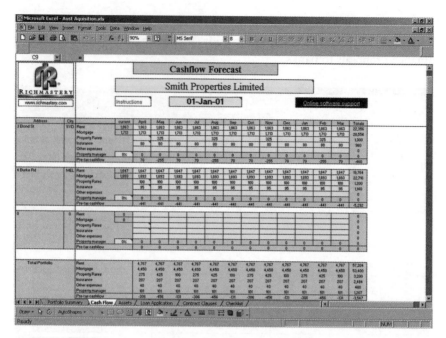

The Cashflow Forecast allows me to detail rental income and all expenses for each property so that I can track the individual performance of each property, whether I own two or 20.

Visit Phil and David's company Leverage Investor Finance. The web site has some great investor services and advice and it is one of the only companies that solely concentrates on providing mortgage finance exclusively to residential property investors. (www.leveragefinance.co.nz & www.leveragefinance.com.au)

▌ What Other Costs Are There?

> You'd be surprised how much it costs to look this cheap.
>
> *Dolly Parton*

There are a host of other costs you need to take into account when making an offer on a property. Factor them into your calculations. They may vary from region to region, but they will nevertheless form part of your transaction.

> It's important to build in all the costs at this stage, because the profit you make from buying and selling Real Estate is determined at the time you buy, not sell. Lock this in to your brain and NEVER forget it.

Here are some of the items you need to factor in:

Legals: I prefer a flat rate deal with my solicitor. And I pay slightly more than I have to, because by doing so I know I'll build a good relationship with the firm in the long run. I also know that, while I might be paying a little more on cheaper properties, I'll be scoring on the expensive ones.

Stamp Duty: (not applicable in New Zealand) This is unavoidable unless you're buying a company. Let me explain. If you are buying a property that happens to be owned by a company, you might be better off buying the company. You see, it's a fairly common practice to set up an investment company purely to buy, and own, a property. If you were to buy the company and the mortgage it has over the property, you'd pay only stamp duty on the nett asset and not the total value of the property. As an example, if a company owned a property worth $1,000,000, but owed $800,000 on it, the company would be worth only $200,000. So, instead of paying stamp duty amounting to some $39,820 on the $1,000,000 property (as you would have to if you bought it in the usual manner), you'd pay only $1,000 in stamp duty on the $200,000 the company was worth. That's a saving of $38,820! You could save even more if you were to approach the mortgagee with the request to release the previous company director's guarantee and

What other costs are there?

substitute it with yours instead (presuming you were secure enough). This way the mortgage would also be transferred into your name, saving you the cost of loan stamp duty and other costs totalling around $12,000. Suddenly, you'd have saved about $50,820.

A word of caution. When purchasing a company from another seller, have your solicitor complete a thorough due diligence to ensure there are no hidden nasty company debts that are likely to come your way after the sale.

Valuation Fees: Most financiers will want a property valuation, so don't waste too much time and effort trying to avoid it. In fact, deliver it to them on a plate. He's what I do.

Phone a valuer (approved by your bank) and commission him to complete a valuation for you. Supply the valuer with all the supporting sales data (your local Real Estate agent will give you this), listing recent comparative house sales in the area and tell the valuer you are still negotiating on the property, but believe the property is worth X amount of dollars.

Usually, the valuer will then deliver you a valuation which is consistent with the amount you consider the property to be worth. Give this valuation to the bank and 95% of the time they will accept it without hesitation.

Loan Application Fees: Try to get these waived, but first make sure there are no early pullout penalties.

Mortgage Insurance: This is usually payable only if you want to get a mortgage that exceeds 80% of the value of the property. If you have a low deposit, this is the cost of doing business.

Building Insurance: I prefer arranging a Blanket Cover for all my properties. It's a cheaper and more convenient way than having a separate policy for each individual property. Negotiate bulk discounts whenever you can.

Contents Insurance: I would recommend you include this in your Building Policy.

Agent's Fees: There are none for buying properties unless you pay finder's fees or commissions to a buyer's agent like www.richmastery.com. But you will have to pay agent's fees when you sell. These are also usually non-negotiable.

Marketing Costs: Most people fail to budget for this. When you do, it will make all the difference when the time comes to sell. You may want to consider placing a few colour advertisements in the local newspapers, designing and printing a brochure (occasionally your Real Estate agent will provide these free of charge, so speak nicely to them), and erecting a large For Sale sign outside the property. There is a cost to effective marketing, but it's worth it for a quick sale. If you use a Real Estate agent to sell your property, they will facilitate getting all your marketing material produced but you will have to pay for it.

Holding Costs: These include items such as interest charges, mowing, and cleaning.

Understand this: These costs are there and need to be covered. If you don't allow for them up front, they will come out of your profit.

▌ Increasing The Value Of The Property

> A wise man should have money in his head, but not in his heart.
>
> *Jonathan Swift*

Increasing the value of your Real Estate investment property is one of the most important aspects to wealth creation. It is the key to unlocking the potential of your property portfolio, so that it can really start working for you.

So how do you go about achieving this?

There's very much more to it than simply refurbishing a property. You see, as I've already mentioned, the biggest trap that awaits most landlords is overdoing things in the hope of making a killing. I can't stress enough how important it is to ensure you don't over-capitalise when you set out to increase the value of your property.

The first thing you need to bear in mind when planning how to achieve an increase in value is to remember the basic reason you bought the property in the first place. By this I mean was it a Quick Cash deal, a Positive Cashflow deal or a Negatively Geared (Capital Growth) deal? This is important because not only must you stick to your game plan, it's important because you'd treat properties in the different categories very differently when it comes to selecting a strategy to increase their value.

Let's consider them separately.

Quick Cash Property Deals

Buy And Sub-Divide, Then Resell Or Refinance

This strategy may seem simple, and it usually is, but there are a few things you need to keep in mind.

Remember, you're working with your local council and other government departments, so do the right thing. Check with them before you embark on any expensive renovation work, as you'll probably need their approval first.

Increasing the value of the property

Many an investor who has failed to do this has learned the hard way by being ordered to undo everything and return the property to how it was before the work began.

There are rules governing what you can and what you can't do when it comes to renovating property. And if it's a unit you are thinking of renovating, you will need to get the approval of the Body Corporate as well, because they too have very specific rules and regulations governing what you can and can't do. These not only incorporate local authority rules, but also the wishes of the other owners of the block or complex.

When it comes to sub-dividing blocks of land, things get a little more complex. Not only are there local government rules that apply, but also the rules vary from suburb to suburb. Inner city areas have rules governing high-density housing and even the type of dwelling you can erect, while the rules governing acreage are quite different. You'll also need to decide whether the blocks will have their own individual facilities like water, electricity, sewerage and storm water drainage, or whether they will be on a common system. If you opt for a common system to save on costs, a Body Corporate structure will need to be set up to look after future maintenance issues.

If you are considering buying a property that you believe falls into this category, my advice is to include a clause in the contract that makes your offer subject to the relevant approvals being given. Allow at least 90 days for this condition to be satisfied.

Don't forget to add in the usual buying and subdivision costs when doing your calculations. These include the following:

- Town Planning costs
- Survey costs
- Registration costs
- Legal costs for the Title
- Sub-division fees
- Council fees
- Sewerage connection costs
- Water, power and phone connection costs
- Contribution to Parks, Wildlife and Environment Levies

Once you have taken care of the costings, and if the deal still stacks up well according to your own goals, objectives and criteria, then ask yourself the following questions before you proceed:

- How will you cover the lack of income while you're sub-dividing the property?
- What's imperative in your negotiations here?
- How can you get the bankers to end-finance this deal for you?
- What could possibly go wrong?
- What sort of Returns On Investment (ROI) are you looking for?
- What else can you do with the extra block of land?

Buy And Change The Use Of, Then Resell Or Refinance

Once again, a simple twist on a very sound strategy. Just keep your eye on the numbers.

Buying well is still paramount, but you need to be able to see what others can't.

The sort of things you might want to do here include the following:
- Convert a large house into room-by-room student accommodation
- Convert flats into Strata Title units (units with completely separate legal titles)
- Buying flats and adding another floor or courtyard to increase rentable space
- Change the floor plan of a block of units
- Change a purpose-built warehouse or squash courts into flats or units

And once again, there are a host of questions you need to answer before proceeding. These include:

- What must you check before you decide to buy anything here?
- What do you need to know about the area before you invest?
- Who should be in charge of the construction and why?
- What could possibly go wrong?
- What sort of Return On Investment (ROI) are you looking for?
- What are the tax and GST implications when you sell?

Positive Cashflow

Build And Rent

Everyone likes a new house. Building a home is part of most individual's great dream. But there are many pitfalls and unless you think your strategy through carefully, you could end up paying far too much for a property. You could also end up being disappointed.

Getting great land is the key to this type of deal. Remember, positive cashflow properties are the ones that will usually only give you average capital gains, but they will always produce massive returns. They are the ones that rent well. You need to ensure that they will attract good tenants – tenants who will be willing to pay above-average rent for it. Ideally the property needs to have an excellent position, be in an excellent location and close to all amenities, come fully equipped and be a better proposition than other properties in the neighbourhood. If you do that you will guarantee a superb rental return, low vacancy rate and maximise the potential of capital growth.

This will have a bearing on the builder you choose and the materials and fittings you use. Remember, home building prices don't vary too much, but a good design will save you plenty.

Some options you may want to consider include the following:

- Buy land and contract a builder to build a new rental property
- Allow for the finishing touches. A tenant expects everything completed
- Buy land and sub-divide to build on each block or keep a block spare

- Buy land for a unit complex or block of flats
- You may like to hold land to build on in slow times

Once again, ask yourself the following questions:

- What should you look for with the land?
- What might you want to include in your negotiations?
- How can you do this with no money down?
- How will you afford the holding costs?
- What sort of returns are you looking for?
- What could possibly go wrong?

Buy Older And Rent After A Tidy Up

This is probably the option most investors take. In fact, this category can be thought of as the Real Estate Investor's Holy Grail. You see, a small and simple tidy up can add another $30 to $50 a week to the rent you can charge.

An increase in rent will result in an increase in the value of your property, making your loan seem small when compared with the property's new valuation.

Here are some of my guidelines for buying properties that fall in this category:

- Buy a solid structure that requires minimal maintenance and a few fix-ups. Maybe doors and windows, a repaint if necessary, perhaps replace the carpets, but most probably a thorough cleanup both inside and out and a day spent in the garden may be all that is required.
- Keep the tidy-up costs to a minimum.

Remember, this is NOT a refurbishment so don't get too carried away. You may also be able to rent the property out straight away and do the tidy up later on. That way at least you'll get your cashflow rolling, and you'll have happy tenants as they'll see you're taking an interest in maintaining the property.

With these properties, you should ask yourself the following questions before you buy:

- What areas should you be looking in?
- How might you bring down the price in your negotiations?
- How much should you limit your budget to?

Increasing the value of the property

- How will you afford the holding costs?
- What sort of return are you looking for?
- What could possibly go wrong?

Buy In Poorer Locations With Higher Rent Returns

Properties that fit into this category make excellent Positive Cashflow properties. But don't fall into the trap of expecting massive capital growth when the time comes for you to sell. That's not why you buy in this category in the first place – your objective is high rental returns. And as an indication of what your returns are likely to be, consider this; units costing around $35,000 will rent for about $95 a week, while houses that cost about $65,000 will rent for $110 a week.

Suburbs that fit the bill here are usually outer suburbs of poor quality or inner suburbs that need rejuvenating. Check to see that both property and tenant insurance is available in the area. Some insurance companies won't provide cover in a few high crime areas.

Just ensure the property is in presentable condition. Don't bother with too much renovation or repair work; properties in this category will rent anyway and provide you with a good return on your investment.

Keep things in perspective, though. Make sure the Property Manager you use credit checks all prospective tenants and checks all tenant blacklists, as the last thing you need is a so-called 'Tenant From Hell'. Choose a tenant that looks after the property; that way you won't have to go overboard with repair or renovation costs on a low cost property. We have found the best tenants are single Mums with kids, gay couples or even young families. They are usually the safest bet.

From a buyer's point of view, buying in this category may look attractive, but there are certain factors you need to bear in mind. You need to ask yourself the following questions:

- What suburbs should you be looking in?
- How will you be sure you're getting a solid deal?
- Why is insurance so important?
- Should you allow for extra vacancy periods or not?
- What sort of returns are you looking for?
- What could possibly go wrong?
- Why are these simple, yet great, deals?

Buy Multiple Dwellings On One Lot

If you are considering buying multiple dwellings on one block, you must bear in mind that although the deal will produce great positive cashflow from all properties, only the ONE BLOCK will be gaining CAPITAL VALUE. This usually takes a little more time, but the lower land cost allows for positive cashflow returns.

The type of properties I am talking about here include the following:

- Two houses on one block, or house A and B.
- Flatettes and Granny Flats – they usually share the toilet/bathroom.
- Boarding houses – you need time to collect the rent or have a live-in manager.
- Serviced rooms – here you need an on-site manager.
- Caravan parks – you'll need an on-site manager.
- Backpacker Hostels – they need on-site managers.

Flats converted to accommodation for overnight stays – these are usually near the beach or hospitals.

Entire blocks of units – they require a higher capital outlay, but offer great cashflow in return.

Once again, you need to go into these deals with your eyes wide open. Ask yourself the following questions before you decide whether to proceed or not:

- What's the one main consideration here?
- Why is it so easy to get positive cashflow here?
- What do you have to remember about vacancy rates?
- Will you get much capital growth, and why?
- What sort of return are you looking for?
- What could possibly go wrong?

Convert To Student Accommodation

Buying near a university, college or a hospital is the first step in this process. Make sure the properties you're considering have lots of bedrooms, as this is the key to getting the most rental income possible.

Increasing the value of the property

If you're considering supplying accommodation to this market, you should only look at properties that have the potential to convert other rooms into bedrooms.

Either you, someone you trust or a good Property Manager will need to collect the rents each month. Or you may be able to get one of the tenants to collect the rent for you and keep the yard tidy in exchange for a small rent reduction.

I'd recommend you consider signing one Head Lease – that way you can avoid having to register as a boarding house, which can cost.

The sort of questions you need to ask when considering buying for this market include:

- Which suburbs should you be looking in?
- How can you get the maximum number of bedrooms?
- How will you price each room?
- What time of the year is best to buy and tenant a property?
- What sort of returns are you looking for?
- What could possibly go wrong?

Negative Cashflow (Capital Growth)

The types of properties that typically fall into this category are ones in a TOP POSITION with ASSURED CAPITAL GROWTH. But understand that growth needs to exceed the cash contributed each week or month to make this type of deal worthwhile. And just because it's negatively geared doesn't mean it can't be cash flow positive.

You are not going to get a positive cashflow property that has huge capital growth very often but they are out there so keep your eyes peeled. I regularly find the only people that can't find positive cashflow capital growth properties are people who don't believe they exist. It never ceases to amaze me how people handicap themselves by their own ignorance.

Look for capital growth properties in top positions like a riverfront or water front, river views or water views, on a hilltop with good views, city views, or adjacent to parklands, state or national forests or reserves. Look for properties that are in unique positions or are unique properties in other ways, be it a high growth coastal resort or in a high class, OLD MONEY suburb.

You will still want to buy well, though, and you won't want to have to do much work to it, if anything. I'd also recommend you buy after a period of no growth or at the bottom of the market, not the top.

100% financing on these types of properties can make it hard to do a deal that's cashflow positive. So it's important you have already stocked your portfolio with some positive cashflow properties so they can subsidise any shortfall in rental income you may incur from the negatively geared (capital growth) property.

Before buying a Negative Cashflow property, you should ask yourself the following questions:

- How do you know the area you're considering is a high growth area?
- What will negotiations be like in this area?
- What forms must you file in this situation?
- What could go wrong?
- What sort of Return On Investment (ROI) are you looking for?

▌ Property Management Techniques

> This house is to be let for life or years; Her rent is
> sorrow, and her income tears. Cupid, 't has long
> stood void; her bills make known, She must be
> dearly let, or let alone.
>
> *Francis Quarles (1592–1644)*

Once you have your investment property, it needs to be properly managed. Good management techniques will maximise your investment return, and this is important because it's the reason you invested in Real Estate in the first place.

When it comes to managing your investment property, you basically have two choices. You can manage it yourself, or you can appoint a professional Property Manager to do this for you.

Presuming you decide on the latter, how do you find a good Property Manager? We've all heard horror stories about incompetent Property Managers who don't care about your property or whether it's vacant for months on end, so what do you do to ensure you don't end up locked into a term contract with a poorly performing Property Manager?

How would you even recognise a good Property Manager from a bad one?

Interview your prospective Property Manager; remember they work for you so treat their appointment with due care and consideration.

- Ask them for references of other investors who have Real Estate in the same area as your property, and phone at least three of the referees!

- Ask them about the area, test their knowledge

- Make sure they credit check all tenants before they rent the property to them. I have saved thousands of dollars in lost rent just by using a Property Manager who does credit checks when my old Property Manager didn't.

- Ask them how often they conduct inspections on the property and what form these reports take.

- Get them to give you a written rental appraisal of your property and what they believe it should rent for. Check this is accurate with several other Real Estate agents who work in the area.

- Ask to see a copy of their monthly management report that gets sent to you each month. What you'll be looking for here is meaningful documentation. Many agents just produce sheets of paper with boxes ticked. These are not good enough. A detailed report to the owner is what I expect.

- Ask how they handle repairs on your property. I have a standing order with my Property Manager that if something needs fixing and it's under $250 they take care of it and don't even bother me. I have to approve any expenditure over $251.

- Check if they pay your rent to you weekly, fortnightly or monthly. Payment weekly or fortnightly is a big bonus because this enables you to minimise any interest you may have on a line of credit account, and it's much better for cashflow!

- Ask how long they have been established and what their experience is.

- Ask to see the tenancy agreements they use and have a good read of it

- And, of course, check their fees. In my experience 7-8% of the rental income is reasonable. Usually the cheapest Property Managers are the worst.

 Make sure the Property Managers contract can be terminated by you within 48 hours should they fail to fulfil the terms of the contract.

Speak to the agent about the techniques they use to ensure vacancy periods are minimised. Ask them about the timing of the commencement and expiry of fixed term lease/rental agreements. Will they open your property for inspection on Sundays? This is preferable, as many tenants would prefer to select a property on the weekend and sign the lease there and then rather than having to take a day off during the week for this.

My Property Manager is excellent! When I buy a property, I advise him, he goes down to the property and views it and then rings me. He advises me that if I replace the carpet, paint the hall, and repair the cracked window (he confirms quoted prices for doing all of this) at a cost of $1276, he can get a weekly rental of $250 instead of $200.

Now you don't have to be a rocket scientist to work out that by spending $1276 I get back $2600. That's a 100+% return on my investment.

His value to me is his expertise and the TIME he saves me, because all I have to do is say, "Yes, make it happen," and he co-ordinates and manages the entire process.

Not only that but because I let him know about my purchase four weeks before I settle on it, he has four weeks to find a great tenant and organises for them to move in on settlement day so I have rent rolling in from day one.

Once I had a truck back into one of my rental properties and take the corner off it. My Property Manager rang me (while I was in the queue at Subway buying lunch). He said: "Just calling to let you know a truck has backed in to your house at xyz St, We have a builder on the way and have organised the claim with the insurance company and the insurance assessor. You don't have to do anything but I thought you might like to know in case you drove past and saw the damage."

Not only was the Subway good, but lunch was all the more enjoyable knowing I had a great player on my team who made playing the game a whole lot easier.

■ Selling Techniques

> Everyone is in business for himself, for he is selling his services, labour or ideas. Until one realizes that this is true he will not take conscious charge of his life and will always be looking outside himself for guidance.
>
> *Sidney Madwed*

Selling Real Estate is all about marketing. If you understand the principles of marketing, you'll be well ahead of everyone out there in the market place, and that includes most of the professionals.

You need to understand clearly the difference between marketing and selling. With selling, you start with the product and then look for someone to sell it to. It's the way business worked long, long ago. It's the old paradigm. Marketing turns this process on its head and starts off with the market – the people they want to sell to. True marketing professionals consider their target market carefully, understanding their needs, requirements and frustrations. They then look for products with which to satisfy these needs. And if they can't find any, they produce them from scratch.

Marketing works well because it is consumer-oriented. Why then when it comes to Real Estate do we naturally want to fall back on out-dated, inefficient and risky selling techniques?

If you've been following the advice given in this book, you won't find yourself falling into this trap because when you bought, you'd have carefully considered who would buy the property from you. You will have taken their needs and requirements into consideration and renovated accordingly. You'll know who your target market is. All you'll have to do is find ways of reaching them.

Develop a database of potential buyers. You know their attributes, so you can develop strategies to reach them. Advertising in the local papers is usually the best method. But what I like to do to maximise my chances of achieving the best price possible is to list the property with an agent in the next best suburb. That's the neighbouring suburb where the average prices are higher than the area in which my property is situated. Here's why.

Buyers looking to buy in their preferred suburb will quickly ascertain what the going prices are in that area. And they'll usually be feeling slightly out of their depth, financially. The local agent will be running them around looking at stock in their chosen price range, and they'll be wondering how much they can knock the prices down. That's human nature, after all. But if the agent senses this opposition to price, my property could be suggested. Generally, mine will be of a higher standard and better quality than the run-of-the-mill stock on the market because I will have specifically renovated it to meet the requirements of these buyers. And it will be considerably cheaper, due to the fact that it is situated just over the suburban boundary. The buyer immediately weighs up the advantages and disadvantages, and the deal swings my way. I also don't have to negotiate on price very often. Sure I encounter buyer resistance in many instances, but I always find a buyer who recognises value for money (my price).

Another technique that isn't used nearly enough is the tender system. Why go to auction if you can basically achieve the same result by putting the property out to tender?

You see, agents sell the auction method by saying it's major advantage lies in the fact that it puts your property on the market without a price. Well, so too does the tender method. You achieve the same end result without having to endure the stress involved with auctions. And, tenders are a lot more honest. At least you'll have something down on paper and you'll know it's there. You can still judge the best offer when the tender closes, but each person who tenders won't know what the others have offered. Tenders are really just silent auctions where you have all the control! You'll end up with more than one offer, whereas with auctions you end up with only one (presuming you get that far).

The other thing I often do when selling a property is to list with the most popular agent in the area. How do I know who that is? Simple. I drive around and see who's most active. I look to see who has the most signs up. It's easy to do; yet most buyers fail to do this. Alternatively, you could phone the local Real Estate Board and get the statistics on which Real Estate office is selling the most Real Estate in your area.

Lease To Purchase Deals

There might be an occasion when you have a property that you are losing money on and you just can't sell. It might be that you thought it a good deal at the time, but since then things have changed. The market could have dropped, or the growth you predicted for the area just hasn't materialised.

What do you do?

One great option is the Lease to Purchase deal.

Lease to Purchase deals are great for other situations too, not just for moving difficult-to-sell stock. They offer fantastic returns with minimal outlay and fuss, and you get the world's best tenant as part of the deal. This is how I do it:

I reserve this type of deal only for people who have no money. Understand this: having no money doesn't mean they are bad risks. Not at all. I am very particular about who I deal with and I go about finding these people very carefully.

I usually start by placing an advertisement in the local paper that reads something like the following:

'Own your own home. No deposit finance available to the right person. Ring....'

or

'Own your own home, $5,000 down and $750 a month'

or

'Vendor Must Sell, No Credit Checks'

One advertisement usually results in around 60 replies. I tell each one that I can help them buy their own home, but I aim to make money along the way. This might weed out half the respondents. You see, I'm looking for a particular group of people here – recently divorced males who are starting out again with a new partner. They have the regular income, and are keen to impress their new partner by giving her security and a good home. They usually can't afford to buy in the normal manner because they probably lost most of their assets as a result of the divorce, but they want to get up and running as soon as possible.

Selling techniques

When I find the right person, I work out a financial package with a low entry deposit and repayments they can afford. If they don't have the deposit they then go and get a small personal loan from the bank or withdraw the amount in cash against their credit card. They must then go and find three homes in that price bracket that they would like to live in. That done, I begin negotiating with the owners until I'm successful with one.

Here's a step-by-step guide of how to do this:

- You buy a property.

- You then become a banker.

- You sell the property on a long-term lease with a low deposit and high repayments.

- Your tenant owns the property, does all maintenance, and takes care of it as if it is their own.

- You collect the margin between your bank repayments and the tenant's repayments to you. This is usually between $100 and $250 a month.

- You have to finance the deal and come up with the deposit to purchase the property.

What can go wrong? Not much, because if the tenant defaults, you take back the house because the title has not yet been transferred. You also have their deposit and they will have looked after the property really well, as in their minds it was their home that they were paying off.

The advantages of Lease to Purchase deals include the huge cashflow they produce, the fact that you have no rental headaches, and the large capital loss you get to write off at the end of term.

There are certain disadvantages, though. You can't have it both ways. You don't get long-term capital growth from these deals, only a very good cashflow. It is also getting harder to finance with some banks that don't like you acting as a middleman.

An example:

Let's assume you've just purchased a unit for $35,000 with $5,000 down as a deposit and $4,000 in costs. Let's also assume your repayments on the $30,000 bank loan are about $220 a month.

You then lease the unit for a $3,000 deposit and $480 a month. I recommend you price the unit at what it would normally rent for plus about 20% to 30%.

You undertake NO CREDIT CHECKS, but always do a blacklist check as you would for any a rental. You don't want to get any nasty surprises further down the track.

Once you have received the deposit from the tenant, you'll have $6,000 in the deal ($5,000 deposit plus $4,000 in costs less the $3,000 down payment) and be making $260 a month. That's $3,120 a year with NO costs and NO hassles. Let's put it another way; you'll be making a return of about 52%.

Think of these deals like the car yard on the corner, where everyone knows that not only will you pay more for cars, but you will also pay a higher rate of interest. But they will sell you a car, no matter what your credit rating.

■ Protecting Your Investment

> The power of hiding ourselves from one another is mercifully given, for men are wild beasts, and would devour one another but for this protection.
>
> *Henry Ward Beecher (1813 - 1887),*
> *"Proverbs from Plymouth Pulpit", 1887*

One of the most effective means of protecting your investments is through the establishment of a firewall. The purpose in doing this is to protect your own private assets as well as any other investment properties you may have in the event one deal turns sour or something unexpected happens.

The establishment of a company and/or trust is the best way to provide firewall protection for investors. If you choose to set up a company to own your investment property, you do need to understand that companies are identities in their own right. And as a director of that company, you have certain legal responsibilities and duties. Trusts can be more flexible because they don't involve other shareholders.

There are various different types of trusts that serve a variety of purposes.

 Important Point: The quality of the Trust Deed is critical to the level of protection a trust enjoys. Make sure you use an accountant or solicitor that is also an Asset Protection Specialist when establishing a trust. DO NOT use your corner dairy accountant or solicitor.

Getting your money out of a trust is far more difficult than getting it out of a company. Companies are more flexible in this regard, because all you need to do is to either sell the company or re-issue shares.

My advice is to seek professional advice regarding the type of structure best suited to your own particular situation. It's a complex field where regulations are constantly changing. Check out the preferred supplier's page at www.richmastery.com

Possible Structures

Investors should carefully weigh the following considerations when they are planning the structure of their Real Estate investments with a suitably qualified Asset Planning Specialist:

- Tax minimization (both personal and company/trust)
- Protection of the family home
- Protection of investments
- Long Term Estate Planning (wills, etc)
- Inheritance (for the children)

There are a myriad of Asset Planning Structures available. Few books are written on this subject because legislation that influences this area is constantly shifting, and the need for individuals to seek professional advice from Asset Planning experts to personalise a structure that meets specific circumstances.

We want to paint a gallery of possibilities so you can have a taste of the benefits as well as a better understanding of the different structures available to enable you to have a much more meaningful discussion with your expert Asset Planning professional.

We are not solicitors or accountants and do not seek to give any form of carte blanche financial advice. Everyone's circumstances are different and your Asset Planning solutions should be solely devised and implemented in consultation with an Asset Planning expert.

This book is your guide to the menu; how you mix the ingredients is totally up to you.

The Menu ...

Sole Trader

A Sole Trader is the name given to individuals who are in business for themselves. The Sole Trader acts alone in business. It is the simplest method of trading with the minimal amount of fuss. There is no asset protection and very little tax advantages.

Partnerships

A partnership is where two or more parties – either people or other entities — combine to achieve a common outcome. Make sure you have a partnership agreement in place before you begin trading, as partnerships generally don't work in the long run. An agreement will help both of you understand the rules and what your aims and objectives are. It will also make it a lot simpler when the time comes for you to part company. Understand this: The only ship that is guaranteed to sink is a partnership!

Companies

A company is a separate legal entity that has its own rights. A company is owned by its shareholders and is managed on a day-to-day basis by its directors. Many property investors use companies to own properties.

Trusts

Trusts can be very effective if set up correctly. But keep in mind that you need some flexibility when establishing them because they often come under scrutiny.

Superannuation Funds

I'm not talking here about the major commercial funds, but the type you might establish and run yourself as a self-employed person – the so-called DIY Super Funds. You need to be aware that there are rules and regulations that govern DIY Funds, and unless you have tens of thousands of dollars in your fund, you're better off sticking with the traditional funds.

Limited Partnerships

These are US partnership arrangements that are not available in Australia. Again, if you are interested in these, consult your solicitor.

Offshore Structure

Offshore structures are, in general, more trouble than they're worth. Leave them alone.

A Typical Investors Structure

When I go about setting up a business structure, the most important consideration I believe I need to bear in mind is FLEXIBILITY. This is important for a number of reasons. Firstly, I want to be able to manoeuvre. I want to be secure in the knowledge that whatever happens in the future, whatever changes the authorities may introduce, my options are not limited or restricted. Secondly, I don't want to be caught out operationally and not be able to finalise a deal because of limitations brought about by my business structure. Thirdly, I want maximum protection, not only in the event something goes wrong with a deal, but if I want to package a deal in a certain way as security when raising finance, I don't want my personal assets being placed at risk. I also don't want one deal to become a risk to the others – I want them to remain isolated from each other.

So, what type of structure would a typical investor have?

They would set up a company and trust structure every time. But understand this: it's better to set a company up with 180 or 1800 shares rather than 2 or 10. It's much more flexible that way. You see, that way you can always sell off shares in the company later, without losing control, and you can issue or sell shares to various individuals on various and differing terms.

An investor would set up a company that has 20 A Class shares and 1800 G Class shares. The A Class shares are management shares while the G Class shares are profit shares. If I am going to sell shares in the company, I NEVER sell A Class shares. I can actually sell all the G Class shares and still retain full control of the company. And by issuing a range of other shares such as E and F Class shares (to the investor's partner or children, for instance) they have maximum flexibility when it comes to allocating profits each year.

The investor would have a structure made up of three entities; two being companies - one the trading company and the other the asset company - and the third being a trust. The trading company does all the work but contains no assets, while the asset company holds all the assets and does no work. The trading company takes all the risk.

This structure is what we put in place for each Property Wealth Wheel. I NEVER include more than one Property Wealth Wheel in one of these structures. The reason for this is that if there is something that goes wrong, I risk losing more than I need to.

How do I transfer money from one Property Wealth Wheel to another? Quite simple. I take money from the Asset Company of the first structure and invest it in Fixed Term Deposits. I then use this as security to raise money for the next Property Wealth Wheel. That way it costs nothing, there are no nasty tax implications and it's quite secure.

Every single loan we have is INTEREST ONLY. I know banks will pressure you to make deposits against the principal as well, because it's this money they use to lend to others. But we resist and will take our business elsewhere if necessary. We usually aim to refinance our properties after two or three years anyway.

▌Common Mistakes

> If I had to live my life again, I'd make the same mistakes, only sooner.
>
> *Tallulah Bankhead (1903 - 1968)*

Like anything else, investing in Real Estate can be anything but plain sailing. Some investors seem to make just about every mistake in the book. Others seem to succeed despite themselves, benefiting more from being in the right place at the right time. In reality, these people are not really investors at all. They're better described as speculators.

The serious investor always takes a planned approach to investing in Real Estate. And so they should because it is, after all, a serious business. That doesn't mean it needn't be fun. In fact, I believe it should be, because you want to sleep at night.

Real Estate is serious business because you need to approach it in a serious way. You need to follow a carefully planned and well thought out strategy based on a set of rules to ensure your chances of making costly mistakes are minimised. Why learn the hard way? Why not heed what others have done before you by taking note of what works and what doesn't?

Investor Pitfalls

After years of experience in the Real Estate market, we've seen investors at all levels continually making the same basic mistakes. There are certain basic pitfalls that snare even the more astute and experienced investor. The good news is they're simple mistakes that are easily avoided. All that's required is a basic awareness of them. They include:

- Over-capitalisation.
- Thinking you're smarter than you actually are.
- Understanding your market.
- Cost blow-out when renovating.
- Time blow-out when renovating.
- No check sheet.

- Pest inspection certificates that don't indicate whether previous pest damage has been rectified.
- Including sufficient clauses on contracts.

What Not To Buy

When you hit the road and begin looking at properties, you also need to bear in mind factors that would rule out a particular property. You need to be able to recognise what kind of property to avoid, not because it may be a dog box, but because it doesn't meet your particular needs at the time. You must be able to recognise something that doesn't fit with your game plan.

As a general rule, we would advise you to stay well clear of properties that fall into the following categories:

- A house you think you might live in at some stage down the track. It could be a house on the coast that you reckon you should buy now and move into when you eventually retire. Don't make the mistake of confusing lifestyle decisions with investment decisions. By all means buy yourself a retirement cottage at the coast – only don't include it with your investment properties.

- Property being marketed by shady marketers who buy the property at one price and sell it to you at an inflated value that bears no relevance to its real market value. These types of deals have received considerable negative publicity, and are best avoided. They are usually easily identified by the agent's promise to fly you interstate to view the property at no cost to yourself.

- Anything where you have to pay full price. By this I do not mean you should never pay the asking price. Understand that if you are after a top-quality property in a top location, you may have to pay a reasonable amount for it. That's the reality. It's simply a question of supply and demand. But I believe these instances will be fairly few and far between. Discount is king!

- A property you fall in love with ... unless you're going to live there a LONG time. Remember what I said about not letting your emotions get in the way of a good deal?

- Anything that puts you into so much debt you can't sleep at night.

- A lot of building value and very little dirt value. The real value in owning Real Estate isn't so much the value of the building (which depreciates over time) but the value of the land (which increases over time). I very seldom hold units long-term for this reason unless they are full blocks where I own the land as well.

- A lot of house value with no suburb or street value. It's often not rewarding owning the very best house in an average street or suburb.

- Anything where the numbers don't work. Otherwise what's the point?

▌Getting Down To Business

> We succeed only as we identify in life, or in war, or in anything else, a single overriding objective, and make all other considerations bend to that one objective.
>
> *Dwight D. Eisenhower (1890 - 1969),*
> *speech, April 2, 1957*

It's now time to start putting what you've read into ACTION. You need to start thinking about your goals and how you are going to achieve them. It's time to get practical.

Here are the eight steps you need to take to get the ball rolling. This is your ACTION PLAN. It's a list of what needs to be done to acquire your first investment property. It's also a major step along the road to wealth and riches.

Step 1. Design your strategy or game.
- What game/s do you want to play?
- Will you play the game at an active or passive level?
- Will you include a business in your strategy?
- Will you trade the Stock Market?
- If so, will it be on a long-term or short-term basis?
- Will you include Real Estate in your game?
- Are you after apartments, houses or blocks of units?
- Will you use a combination of the above?
- What playing field will you play on … and in what area?

Step 2. Develop your investment rules.
- What are your RULES for each game you've decided to play?
- What are your Return On Investment rules (plus and minus)?
- What are your Portfolio Management rules?
- What are your re-investing rules?
- What are your time and effort rules?

Getting down to business

Step 3. Decide on your outcome or goals. Start with a timeframe and end result.
- Re-visit your calculated Return On Investment needed for your outcome.
- Set clear goals for each area of the game.
- Set a reasonable timeframe for each area.
- Will this outcome give you time for a life as well as a good financial result?

Step 4. Develop your plan of ACTION.
- What are the major steps towards your goals going to be?
- How often and how many of each type of property deal will you need to do?
- What sort of profits will your business need to make?
- How many businesses might you need to buy/sell?
- How much will you need to invest from each pay cheque?
- How will you need to set up your structure?
- What people do you need to add or remove from your team of friends, advisers and employees?

Step 5. Look at 50 properties.
- Will you do this fortnightly, monthly, bi-monthly or quarterly?
- How long will you need to actually go and see them physically?
- When will you do this each week?
- What areas, or suburbs, will you go to for each type of deal?
- How many agents will you need to call to get to see 50?
- Use the Property Checklist ... every time. It's part of the Richmastery Acquisition Software available at www.richmastery.com

Step 6. Make offers on ten properties.
- Rustle the bushes as often as you can.
- You're not buying; you're shaking the tree.
- How do you not lose money when putting up $500 per deal?
- How will you pick your price?
- Which ten should you make offers on?
- Remember the terms ... what are the top five terms you'll use?

Step 7. Negotiate a YES on three of them.
- You won't always get a YES; you'll most often get a counter offer.
- Operate on strict numbers ... but don't miss a great deal for $500.
- Remember, if the seller says YES, it doesn't mean you've bought it.
- Understand you're dealing with people who genuinely want to sell.

Step 8. Get finance for one of them.
- Not every deal will get financed.
- Complete a full proposal, with a photograph.
- Use the Richmastery Property Analysis and Acquisition Software as often as possible – it's fantastic and will do everything from predicting when you should buy another property to providing full financial statements. It's available from www.richmastery.com
- Be clear that not every banker will love every deal you do.
- How will you give yourself a great chance to get financing every time?
- What should you be sure to put into your proposal for finance?

Why is it important to look at 50 properties? And how long is that going to take?

Well actually, you can easily do it in a day. But here's a tip. Get yourself a reasonable digital camera and take photos of each place. That way you will be able to remember them when you get back home that night. I download them into a special file in my computer. I would also recommend you invest in a copy of the UBD guide on disc or similar, available from www.ubd.com.au or www.ubd.co.nz. This is invaluable when it comes to considering the properties, because it will show you the area, where the facilities are and where negative factors like municipal dumps or industrial areas are situated.

Get Into ACTION

We've now given you all the knowledge you need to make a huge success from investing in Real Estate. We've shown you what can be achieved and how you can do it. We know it works, because we've done it hundreds of times over. We have guided hundreds, if not thousands, of people just like you to reaching their financial dreams through Real Estate using this knowledge.

Getting down to business

We believe in keeping things SIMPLE, and as a result, our system is not only simple to understand, it's SIMPLE to implement and SIMPLE to manage.

Yet no matter how much we show you how you can reach your financial goals, unless you take this on board and do something with it, nothing will happen. It's now over to you ...

Words can inspire, thoughts can provoke, but only *ACTION* truly brings you closer to your dreams.

Get into *ACTION*.

■ Appendix 1

Tips

The Rule of 72

To work out how long it will take to double your money, divide 72 by the interest rate.

The 1.6 Rule

If the weekly rent (per 1000) is 1.6 times the purchase price, the property will pay for itself. For example, if the purchase price is $100,000, the rent must be $160 a week to pay for itself.

Weekly Rental should be greater than or equal to the Purchase Price divided by 1000 x 1.6

Balancing numbers

If you're trying to balance some figures and you're out by a number that is exactly divisible by 9, then you've written a number down back to front. You might have written 12,367 instead of 12, 376.

Adding value to your property

For every $10 extra you get for weekly rental, you should add an extra $5,200 to the valuation of your property.

Real Estate Agents

If I'm buying property, I deal with the local agent for the area, but if I'm selling, I use one located one or two suburbs up in value. You see, this way my property will be exposed as a red-hot property to buyers in that area.

Self-management

The easiest way to manage yourself is to put a value on your time. Stop doing tasks that cost less than your value to get done. Learn to let go and delegate.

Insuring your future income

Put your money to work first, and then spend what it makes.

Appendix 1

Conveyancing

This is the process of completing and settling on a sale agreement for a property.

Never ever, under any circumstances, do your own conveyancing. It's really not expensive, and being a highly specialised field, it's simply too risky to do yourself.

▌ ABOUT THE AUTHORS –

Bradley J Sugars

Brad is an entrepreneur for many reasons. By the time he was just 28 years of age he was the International Chairman of a global franchise that he started with NO capital. He had his first business at age 15, made a lot of money by the age of 22, lost it all by 22¹/₂, then paid back all his debts and financially retired at 26.

At the age of 15 he employed his friends as paper delivery boys and gleaned a few dollars for the papers they delivered. Since then his businesses have become a little more sophisticated, yet still based on the same principle of finding something people want to buy then selling it to them, making sure he charged well, and gave great service.

By the time he'd finished University, he had completed a Bachelor of Business-Accounting and worked in 27 different jobs; from gardener to pipe maker, pizza cook to radio announcer, and disc-jockey to accounts clerk. One thing he'd definitely learnt; very few people ever really gave anything their best.

As soon as he'd left Uni he got a job selling and invested every single dollar he earned into training himself. Courses on money, investing, sales, business, personal growth - you name it, he did a course in it. He knew that to achieve what he wanted out of life wasn't going to be about how hard he worked, but about how much he knew. By the time he was 21, he was running four retail stores and a photocopy management contract, earning a salary of $60,000 a year.

His mum almost had a heart attack when he told her that he had quit to go and work for himself. Being young and naive was probably a good thing. No capital, but a lot of smart ideas on how to create sales, how to market and how to lead a team of people. By the way, those retail stores increased profits by 39% in the nine months he was in charge.

He bought into a ladies fashion store, a 33% holding with no money down; just the ability to help them create sales. He increased sales by 93% over the first nine weeks and sold his interest back to the other partners just three months later. He did the same with a pizza manufacturing business; he took their product from just being sold into cafes and got it on the shelves of Woolworths, and almost every other small retailer in Queensland. He funded this growth with his earnings from the ladies wear store and was also doing some business consulting in his spare time.

About the authors

It was this consulting that really led him to where he is today. One gentleman he offered his services to *(he used to give away two hours of his time for free, just so people could understand what he could do for them)* ran an international training company. This gentleman, Robert Kiyosaki, a best selling author, asked him to come and train his seminar promoters in the art of marketing. Little did he know then what was in store for him.

Training 30 seminar promoters in Hawaii meant that he was bound to go into the presenting business. Seminars in Hong Kong, New Zealand and in Melbourne meant the sale of the pizza business to create an international operation training and consulting to business owners and managers. Robert asked him to train at his Business School for Entrepreneurs in Hawaii later that year. That was July 1994, and 350 business owners from around the world, 11 trainers (mostly in their 40's and 50's) were there to learn from Brad. He found a business partner who could take care of the operations back home while he got out and presented seminars, did consulting and basically generated the cashflow. And that he certainly did with hundreds of seminars, as many plane flights all over Australia, New Zealand, Asia and into the UnitedStates resulting.

He arrived home in January 1995 to find not only was he was not only tired, sick of travel, and missing regular business, but he was also broke. Major business lesson number one; partnerships don't always work. What to him was VERY serious debt caused him to move back into his parents house, get a phone line connected, put a desk next to his bed and start all over again.

He almost went and got a job. And, as he'd just spent the last 11 months teaching everyone else how to make money (and getting great results for them), he spent three full days just sitting quietly wondering why he couldn't seem to do the same for himself. At the time he thought that life could never get any worse.

He sent a letter to every one of his past clients, seminar attendees and everyone else he knew, offering his consulting services again. And, after a few solid days on the phone, he was back in business. He sat down and wrote out the Vision, Mission and Culture Statement of the new company he was going to create. He decided to stay in the business of training business owners, but this time he'd be sure to do it well.

In March of that year his best friend from University began working with him. They worked from Brad's parents' 'granny flat'. Brad recorded sets of tapes while doing the seminars, kept selling and consulting during the day, and continued selling the tapes. They stayed back until about 10 or 11 each night planning and systemising.

It wasn't long before he'd paid back everything, saved a few dollars, and had a plan in place to create an amazing worldwide organisation. To cut a long story short, within three years and after many trials and tribulations, he managed to create a company called *ACTION International.* Employing 24 people in Australia, they took care of the business in Australia and New Zealand. A joint venture deal (worth several millions of dollars) was then signed to open an office in Singapore to service South East Asia and in 1998 he took the big decision to go global through franchising. 188,000 people had attended *ACTION* seminars by then, 14,300 had been through their intensive workshops, and 397 had benefited from *ACTION* consulting services.

Brad Sugars is currently the Managing Director and CEO of *ACTION International* **Pty Ltd**, as well as Chairman of the *ACTION* Group of Companies around the globe.

Brad is available for a limited number of speaking engagements each year. If you are interested in booking Brad as a keynote speaker for your next annual conference or business event, call *ACTION International* on +61 (7) 3368 2525. It's literally guaranteed that your attendees will say he's "the best speaker we've ever had," time and time again.

David Hows

David has an extensive background in general management and investment. At the age of 16 he joined the Management Training Programme of a large supermarket chain, and progressed through the business over an 8-year period in both store management and head office roles.

David joined a fashion retail group in 1994 and spent the next 4 years in general management roles. In 1998 he joined a large fashion retailer, as retail director, to manage their store operations and supply chain systems for 28 stores. At the same time he completed a number of Post Graduate Diploma in International Business papers. In February 2001 he was headhunted to manage 25 stores, 600 employees and tens of millions of dollars in annual sales for a large multi-national retailer as Regional Sales Manager.

David has always had a desire for excitement and adventure; he is a passionate sailor and a qualified pilot.

David developed a fascination for property and business investment at a young age. After number of years reading all the books he could find on the subject, coupled with numerous international investors' training courses and Entrepreneurs' boot camps, he leaped into his first investment property deal in January 2000.

18 months later he had a large investment portfolio that included numerous residential and commercial properties, along with a multitude of businesses. He then resigned from his day job to pursue investing full time and to teach others the secrets he had discovered that had created his success.

With David's unique investment strategy he rarely puts $1 into a deal!

Phil Jones

Phil has an extraordinary mix of business, property and entrepreneurial skills. At 21 he was headhunted by a struggling communications company to assist with establishing and growing the business. His direct involvement in key management and sales and marketing areas resulted in massive company growth. Over the following 9 years, he acted as the company's corporate troubleshooter, sweeping into deficient areas of the company and going through them like a dose of salts. His mission was to repair, restructure, relaunch and release.

In June 1997 Phil purchased a near death security company with mounting debts that had been horribly mismanaged and was about to be wound up by the Tax Department. At the time of purchase the company employed 1 person full time. 20 months later, the company was experiencing outstanding growth and profit and employed more than 30 staff.

Early in 2000 Phil embarked on a worldwide search for the tools, answers and structures that would deliver him massive financial success. Over the following year and a half he learnt how to create wealth from some of the world's best teachers. And by putting this information into action he created extraordinary property, business and stock market portfolios that have delivered him a financially abundant life.

A dynamic teacher and passionate property investor. Phil now chooses to spend much of his time sharing with others the strategies and processes that changed his life.

▌ Richmastery

The Entrepreneurs Success Centre (www.richmastery.com) was created by Phil Jones and David Hows to empower, inspire and equip investors and entrepreneurs for success.

After completing their own personal journey and going from employees to Multi-millionaires in 3 years, Phil & David understood the process for creating true wealth and financial freedom was simple. The problem was the information on how to do it was uncoordinated, hard to find, poorly delivered, and in a range of different places.

www.richmastery.com was launched to help you shortcut the worldwide search for riches that Phil and David pursued so that you could have one place to visit that provides all of the information, advice, resources and answers you need. Its goal is to serve you with the latest ideas, the finest resources, and the most successful secrets, fresh each day so that you have the tools to be at the cutting edge and the skills to go over it.

Richmastery gives you the...... **The POWER to Change!**

■ RECOMMENDED READING LIST

ACTION INTERNATIONAL BOOK LIST

" The only difference between YOU now and YOU in 5 years time will be the people you meet and the books you read ..." Charlie 'tremendous' Jones

"And, the only difference between YOUR income now and YOUR income in 5 years time will be the people you meet, the books you read, the tapes you listen to, and then how YOU apply it all ..." Brad Sugars

- The E-Myth Revisited by Michael E. Gerber
- My Life in Advertising & Scientific Advertising by Claude Hopkins
- Tested Advertising Methods by John Caples
- Building the Happiness Centered Business by Dr. Paddi Lund
- Write Language by Paul Dunn & Alan Pease
- 7 Habits of Highly Effective People by Steven Covey
- First Things First by Steven Covey
- Awaken the Giant Within by Anthony Robbins
- Unlimited Power by Anthony Robbins
- 22 Immutable Laws of Marketing by Al Reis & Jack Trout
- 21 Ways to Build a Referral Based Business by Brad Sugars
- 21 Ways to Increase Your Advertising Response by Mark Tier
- The One Minute Salesperson by Spencer Johnson & Larry Wilson
- The One Minute Manager by Spencer Johnson & Kenneth Blanchard
- The Great Sales Book by Jack Collis
- Way of the Peaceful Warrior by Dan Millman
- How to Build a Championship Team - 6 Audio tapes by Blair Singer
- Brad Sugars "Introduction to Sales & Marketing" 3 hour Video
- Leverage - Board Game by Brad Sugars
- 17 Ways to Increase Your Business Profits booklet & tape by Brad Sugars. FREE OF CHARGE to Business Owners

*To order products from the recommended reading list call *ACTION International* on +61 (7) 3368 2525

Get Stacks of CASH and Heaps of CUSTOMERS ...

... get your ads designed by our Champion Creative Team ...

As you've just seen there's a lot to remember when it comes to writing effective ads. Well imagine having a team of marketing professionals design your ads for you ...

You will have some of the best in the country writing and designing your ads for you. Professionals who have created thousands of profitable advertisements and marketing campaigns.

Imagine having a Yellow Pages ad that has your phone ringing off the hook, or a Print Ad that has customers flocking through your door. Maybe you'd like an irresistible Sales Script that make prospects feel compelled to buy, or a Referral Strategy that generates hundreds of qualified, cost effective new leads. Our team of copywriters and graphic artists can give you all this and more ...

You can have our Champion Creative Team design a Web-site that will have the orders flooding in, or a Direct Mail campaign that turns your mail box into an amazing profit generating centre. If you're looking to change your image, imagine having our Champion Creative Team design your new Corporate Image or Logo. Best of all we give you a dozen variations on your ads for you to test and measure, so you can be sure to find one that gets amazing results.

Our team is not focussed on being 'clever' or winning awards. For years they've honed their skills in creating campaigns with one goal in mind ... Making Our Clients MONEY.

Being in business is not about doing it all yourself, it's about Leverage. It's about getting outside professionals doing the work for you, so your time is free to focus on growing your business and reaping the rewards. So why spend hours trying to design ads yourself, when you can have our creative team put together a sales and profit focused campaign that will have the money rolling in, in no time.

Call our team TODAY on 1800 670 335, and have us get started on your MONEY MAKING Campaign.

Millionaire In Training

90% of the stuff in this book is missing from most of the wealth creation manuals which are available on the market today ...

Designed to save aspiring Entrepreneurs a lot of mistakes, Billionaire In Training provides an essential framework for creating business success including strategies for increasing profit; a how-to guide for buying, selling and keeping businesses, how to keep yourself on track and moving toward your goals, the 5 Levels of an Entrepreneur and how to advance yourself to the upper levels.

AUD $29.95
(Incl. GST)

Cash, Customers and Ads That Sell

149 Hints, Tips and Strategies on writing Ads that Sell

Armed with all of Brad's super powerful advertising hints and tips, you'll be ready to write super profitable ads in no time at all ...

With Cash, Customers and Ads that Sell, you'll quickly learn how to create profitable strategies and then how to create the ads that make the strategies work ... You'd be mad to pass up the opportunity to get this book.

AUD $29.95
(Incl. GST)

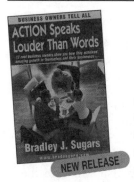

ACTION Speaks Louder Than Words

This book is about ordinary business people achieving astonishing results through business coaching. It chronicles the experiences of 17 businesses and outlines how they achieved phenomenal growth. You'll discover that the only real way to achieving amazing results for your business lies through business coaching. And you'll see it doesn't matter what type of business you run, how old or new your business is, how small or big, or even in what economy you're operating in, coaching can produce unimaginable results.

AUD $29.95
(Incl. GST)

Leverage:
The Game of Business

The rewards start flowing the moment you start playing ...

Leverage is a educational breakthrough that'll have you quickly racking up the profits.

AUD $295.00
(Incl. GST)

The principles you take from playing this game will set you up for a lifetime of business success. It'll alter your perception and open your mind to what's truly possible. Sit back and watch your profits soar.

NEW RELEASE

$ales Rich Video Series

Now you can learn the sales secrets that allowed Brad Sugars to financially retire at the age of 26. And, unlike most gurus, he started with NOTHING.

AUD $495.00
(Incl. GST)

Take advantage of the only multi-millionaire who will teach you exactly how he did it. In this six-video set, Brad gives you more than just theory; he gives you practical step-by-step instructions to take you from being just an average sales person to becoming a SALES SUPERSTAR. And all for just $495.

Billionaire In Training Video

Whether you've read the book or not, you've just got to view this video. Watch Brad Sugars in action as he fires up his audience, imparting powerful business secrets in an easy-to-understand fashion.

AUD $59.00
(Incl. GST)

Not only will you find this best-selling video great value at $59, you'll find it very informative and highly entertaining. It's no wonder he's widely regarded as one of the world's leading business speakers.

Instant Cashflow
(Revised Edition)

Now you can learn Brad's most amazingly powerful and user-friendly sales and marketing tips all in one book.

This book will complement everything you will learn at Brad's Seminar. You will read this book once, then refer to it again and again!

There are so many simple, easy and ready-to-use tips on how to boost your bottom line that you'll have to refer it to your family and friends as well.

AUD $29.95
(Incl. GST)

Instant Leads

One of the fundamental problems most businesses face is the generation of new leads. Without a constant supply of leads, they're faced with a never-ending battle to generate sufficient cashflow for the business to survive from one month to the next.

This book is designed to give you the inside track on everything you need to know about how to generate more leads for your business. It aims at providing you with an INSTANT guide on how to produce the various lead generation tools just like the professionals.

AUD $29.95
(Incl. GST)

Instant Sales

By reading this book, you'll discover the secrets of selling. You'll also discover that the sales process actually starts well before you get to the stage of meeting your prospect face-to-face. You may even be surprised to discover this process actually starts with YOU.

In this book, Brad Sugars explains how to maximise your Conversion Rate, or to put it another way, how to make sure your prospects actually buy from you. He also explains some not-so-well-known techniques that are aimed at smoothing your path through the sales process.

AUD $29.95
(Incl. GST)

NEW RELEASE

AUD $29.95
(Incl. GST)

Instant Promotions

Brad Sugars knows a thing or two about promoting a business. Learn his secrets and follow his easy-to-understand and simple-to-implement steps to promotional success that will put your business on the map.

This book is designed to give you the inside track on everything you need to know about promoting your business. It aims to provide you with an INSTANT guide on how to produce the various promotional items just like the professionals. Once you've read the book, you'll know precisely what it takes to successfully promote your business.

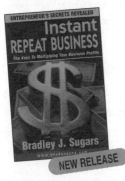

NEW RELEASE

AUD $29.95
(Incl. GST)

Instant Repeat Business

Hanging on to an existing customer is far easier, and much cheaper, than looking for new ones. Yet few business people realise this.

This book is all about looking after repeat business. It's all about ensuring your existing client-base remains happy, loyal and content. It's all about ensuring you look after that 20% of your customer-base that accounts for 80% of your turnover. It's all about turning your existing customers into your most prized asset – Raving Fans.

▋ Double or Triple Your Profits Over the Next 12 Months ...

... and actually work less than half the hours you're currently working ...

This is the most important business workshop you'll ever attend ...

Take your business, whether it's running profitably, making a loss, or even just the seed of an idea and invest 5 days learning and applying strategies that will make you a marketing master. You'll leave the program with a bunch of strategies and ideas that will have your business flying. PLUS, you'll leave with a heap of ads and letters ready to generate real cash for you the moment you get back to your business.

Over the 5 days of Brad Sugars' MARKETING OVERHAUL WORKSHOP you'll discover the most powerful formula for creating cashflow in the world of business. You'll cover more than 70 different ways to generate leads. We will show you dozens of ways to increase the response to your advertising, and actually manage to spend less than you're currently spending.

You'll discover how to increase your conversion rate. It's great to get more enquiries, but it's pointless if you don't make sales. With just a couple of simple techniques you'll be able to sell to more people, without ever needing to offer a discount, or cut into your margins.

You'll probably also like to hear the 5 easiest ways to get your customers coming back more often. I'll take a moment to show you why this one simple idea can be the difference between a business that makes money, and one that goes to the wall. Imagine being able to get each customer spending more when they come into your business. You'll get 53 different strategies, any number of which could increase your cash flow overnight.

We'll also have a talk to you about your margins. It's one thing to have a good turnover, but at the end of the day, we're in business to make money. I'll let you in on 67 strategies that we've used in the past to help business owners make more out of each sale. PLUS you'll learn how to leverage yourself out of your business so you can start working 'ON' your business rather than 'IN' it. You'll also learn how to attract, motivate and keep top class employees.

The MARKETING OVERHAUL WORKSHOP will do more than simply teach you a few marketing strategies. It will give you the mindset of success, and the tools to achieve your business goals. If you want to get ahead of the pack you MUST attend this workshop.

Places in this course are strictly limited. To reserve your place call ACTION International TODAY. *ACTION International* Australia and New Zealand +61 (0)7 3368 2525

Free call within Australia 1800 670 335

Free call within New Zealand 0800 440 335

Singapore and Asia +(65) 221 0100

United States of America (888) 483 2828

Canada (403) 259 5546

■ Real Money Real Estate

Board Game ... Coming Soon

Register your interest in knowing more about the **Real Money Real Estate Board Game** when it is released by sending an email with your contact details to:

boardgame@richmastery.com

This book has been packed full of information that is designed to assist you to become a successful Real Estate investor. But until now we haven't been able to help you put the information in this book into *ACTION*. That's way we have designed the: **Real Money Real Estate Board Game.**

The **Real Money Real Estate Board Game** takes the knowledge from this book and combines it with a challenging multi-dimensional, high intensity, multi-player Real Estate game that will take you to the *next level* of Real Estate investing.

This book gives you the EDUCATION, the game will teach you how to put it into ACTION and blow your mind with the possibilities that await you in the *real* market.

The **Real Money Real Estate Board Game** will teach you powerful lessons that no book can because of its sophisticated multi-level interactive architecture!

So if you're ready for the ultimate Real Estate learning experience and want to go to the next level in your Real Estate investing, register your details now by emailing:

boardgame@richmastery.com

and get set to transform your life with the lessons you will learn from the **Real Money Real Estate Board Game**

Entrepreneurs Training, Where You Discover How to Make Your Wildest Dreams a Reality ...

And, here's why we won't let most people attend this training program...

Never before has there been a workshop like this. Presented by entrepreneur and marketing guru Brad Sugars, this workshop will teach you everything you'll ever need to know about personal wealth, lifestyle and business success. It will change your life in the most positive way imaginable.

The Entrepreneurs Training is not open to everyone. In fact, it's open only to those who share a common goal - the desire to succeed.

Whether you're looking to make the most of your personal wealth, or increase the cashflow of your business, this 5 day, live-in workshop, will provide you with memorable gifts that will remain with you for the rest of your life.

This workshop is strictly invitation only. You'll need more than just money and time to attend this course. You'll need to embrace the workshop's motto - 'Whatever it takes'. 100% full on from the word go, you'll work hard, play hard and learn the level of performance you'll need to work at to create the entrepreneurial success you're after ...

If you could imagine what it would be like to achieve everything you've ever dreamt of, and have 100% trust in yourself, you'll understand why the Action Entrepreneurs Training is strictly Employees Not Allowed. You can never live in a state of fear, or work from an unleveraged place again after you've lived through these 5 days ...

You don't make a fortune running businesses, you make a fortune selling them. Discover how to take every business you have and turn it into capital growth. Unlike property, shares or any other form of investment, you can massively increase the value of your investment in a very short space of time, reaping the rewards both along the way and when you sell.

This workshop will do more than simply teach you how to make money. It's about discovering who you are, and who you want to be. You're guaranteed to get more out of The Entrepreneurs Workshop than any other workshop you've been to in the past.

This workshop is an absolute must. Call *ACTION* International TODAY to reserve your place. *ACTION* International Australia & New Zealand +61 (0)7 3368 2525

▌ ACTION Contact Details ...

Action International **Australia**

Ground Floor, ACTION House, 2 Mayneview Street, Milton QLD 4064

Ph: 61 (0) 7 3368 2525

Fax: 61 (0) 7 3368 2535

Free Call: 1800 670 335

Action International **Asia**

171 Tras Street, #08-177 Union Building, Singapore 079025

Ph: 65 (0) 6 221 0100

Fax: 65 (0) 6 221 0200

Action International **Europe**

Office 407, MWB Business Exchange, 26-28 Hammersmith Grove, London W6 7BA

Ph: 44 (0) 208 600 1874

Fax: 44 (0) 208 834 1100

Action International **North America**

5670 Wynn Road Suite C, Las Vegas, Nevada 89118

Ph: 1 (702) 795 3188

Fax: 1 (702) 795 3183

Free Call: (888) 483 2828

ACTION Offices around the globe:

**Australia I Canada I China I England I France I Guatamala I Hong Kong
India I Indonesia I Ireland I Malaysia I Mexico I New Zealand I Phillipines
Scotland I Singapore I USA I Wales**

■ ATTENTION BUSINESS OWNERS ...
increase your business profits

Here's how you can have one of Brad's *ACTION* Business Coaches guide you to success...

Like every successful sporting icon or team, a business needs a coach to help it achieve it full potential. In order to guarantee your business success you can have one of Brad's teams as your business coach. You will learn about how you can get amazing business results with the help of the team at *ACTION International.*

The business coaches are ready to take you and your business on a journey that will reward you for the rest of your life. You see, we believe *ACTION* speaks louder than words.

Complete & post this card to discover how the team at *ACTION* can help you increase your income today...

*ACTION International...*Business Trainers and Consultants... ...Because being in business should give YOU more life...

Name . . . .

Position . . . .

Company . . . .

Address . . . .

. . . .

Phone . . . .

Fax . . . .

E-mail . . . .

Referred by . . . .